NEVER ON A

NEVER ON A

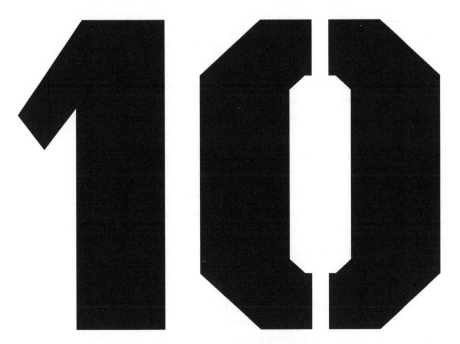

ONE FIREFIGHTER'S POWERFUL (AND SOMETIMES HUMOROUS) MEMOIRS OF

20 YEARS IN THE BUSIEST FIREHOUSES IN NORTH AMERICA

BOB PALESTRANT

MIAMI-DADE COUNTY FIRE RESCUE, FL (RET.)

Printed in the United States of America.
First paperback edition May 2023.

Cover and layout design by G Sharp Design, LLC.
www.gsharpmajor.com

ISBN: 979-8-9882291-1-7 (paperback)
ISBN: 979-8-9882291-0-0 (hardcover)
ISBN: 979-8-9882291-2-4 (ebook)

This book is dedicated to my wife Carol,
whose extraordinary combination of common sense and
intuition keeps me on the right track.

CONTENTS

PART IV: TIMING IS EVERYTHING

INTRODUCTION

Firefighters are not heroes: at least not the way the media has portrayed us in movies and television shows. We don't run on noteworthy calls every day, but when a gripping multiple alarm building fire requiring dozens of firefighters and units to respond, or a horrific mass casualty incident due to a terrorist attack occurs, we know we have to be physically and mentally ready to go 24 hours a day. Sometimes, even that is not enough.

According to the National Fire Protection Association (NFPA 2020), firefighters and paramedics in the United States responded to over 36,000,000 calls for service each year. Due to a myriad of requests for assistance, they must be proficient in the language arts, and have a fundamental knowledge of math and the sciences, particularly chemistry. Furthermore, firefighters must wear multiple hats: they are a combination of contractors, engineers, electricians, carpenters, and plumbers as they must consistently deal with construction-related issues on fire-related or collapse incidents. To that end, a working knowledge of hydraulics and arson investigation are also necessities. Additionally, due to the inability of many to be able to pay for or have transportation to health service facilities, they are time and time again the primary healthcare providers for most of the population.

When dealing with medical and/or fire related calls, South Florida is a microcosm of many of the urban areas across this great country. Unlike most areas however, the population centers of Miami-Dade, Broward and Palm Beach Counties are one contiguous metropolitan area. Although there are markers identifying county and city boundary lines, there are no discernible signs to distinguish a change from one municipality to the next. The almost 70 fire departments serving the residents and visitors of these three counties alone responded to close to 2,000,000 calls for assistance in 2020.

Most front-line firefighters in South Florida work 24-hour shifts with 48-hours off. This includes weekends, holidays, special occasions, and other days those outside public safety take for granted. When not responding to structure or vehicle fires, firefighters in South Florida respond to emergencies of all types; from cardiac and respiratory failure, motor vehicle accidents, childbirths, and gunshot and stab wounds. They evacuate stretcher-bound patients before and during tropical storms and hurricanes, and staff shelters during those storms, away from their families for days at a time.

They provide CPR, first aid, and fire extinguisher training classes, Community Emergency Response Team (CERT) training, and participate in career days at public, charter, and private schools. Firefighters perform pre-fire planning in educational facilities, hospitals, commercial and industrial structures in order to protect the public they serve. They conduct fire inspections, and regularly review current fire science and emergency medical services literature to keep their skills current. There are continual in-service and hands-on training sessions to maintain firefighting and medical rescue skills; responses to water-related emergencies including dives in 60 to 80-foot rock pits with zero visibility, debris and disease-laden canals, or alligator-filled lakes.

They promote themselves as "sex symbols" on firefighter calendars in order to raise hundreds of thousands of dollars for multiple local charities including the Miami Project to Cure Paralysis, Habitat for Humanity's Hurricane Andrew Fund, Ronald McDonald Children's Charities, Neighbors 4 Neighbors, Best Buddies, Cystic Fibrosis, Here's Help, and Safe Haven for Newborns.

They have given their lives serving the citizens of South Florida in too many ways; drowning trying to pull a young girl out of car in a canal, electrocuted while trying to save someone in a vehicle accident while off-duty, dying from the after-effects of hazardous chemicals seeping into their lungs, and killed less than one month from retirement trying to save a businessman's property from burning to the ground.

Over two dozen firefighters working for Miami-Dade County and the City of Miami Fire Rescue Departments alone have died of brain tumors over the past two decades; a 32% higher rate than the national average. According to the Firefighters Cancer Foundation, firefighters have a 53% greater chance of developing Multiple Myeloma, 51% for Non-Hodgkin's Lymphoma, and 102% of developing testicular cancer. Even with the most advanced technological safety equipment available, unbeknownst to the public, the national average life span for firefighters after retirement is approximately eight years.

These statistics do not include the elevated rate of suicides and/or attempts that have been linked with posttraumatic stress disorder (PTSD), (Stanley, et al. 2015).

The loss of friends and colleagues in the Fire Service such as Indy Morgado, Manny Morales, Steve English, Freddy Figueredo, Carlos Lewis, Dewey Henry, Clyde Porter, Brian Gaughan, and Chris Zargo as well as many others has had a profound effect on my life and made me appreciate our time together that much more.

Hopefully this provided a realistic overview of who we are and what we do, not how we are portrayed on television.

PART I: THE JOB

"SETTING THE STAGE"

I had what I considered the greatest career in the world: Professional Firefighter. Those two words symbolize everything about the occupation, both for those in the profession and those who aspire to be part of it. Edward Croker, the Chief of the Fire Department of New York (FDNY) from 1899-1911, was quoted as saying, "I have no ambition in this world but one, and that is to be a fireman. The position may, in the eyes of some, appear to be a lowly one; but we who know the work, which the fireman has to do believe that his is a noble calling. Our proudest moment is to save lives. Under the impulse of such thoughts, the nobility of the occupation thrills us and stimulates us to deeds of daring, even of supreme sacrifice" (Croker, 1910).

To me, it is typified by the lasting image of firefighters bringing victims out of a burning building, performing CPR on someone's grandmother, or carrying a small child out of the remains of a building attacked by terrorists in Oklahoma City. It is the embodiment of someone standing at an intersection for eight to ten hours collecting loose change and dollar bills to continue the fight against muscular dystrophy, or for donations to the local burn center while still responding to twenty to thirty calls on a Saturday or Sunday. It is the school or community center demonstration, career day presentation, or the collection for needy families during Thanksgiving or Christmas. I had seen firefighters on the local, national and international news almost daily, and constantly saw the trucks going on calls, but I didn't quite realize what the term Professional Firefighter meant until I became one.

I was working as a Registered Nurse in a local hospital emergency department and knew close to fifty firefighters from both then Metro-Dade County Fire Rescue (MDFR) and the City of Hialeah, a municipality in the northwest section of the county. Almost daily, one or two of them would say, "Bob, take the test: you have no idea what you're missing. It's the best job in the world."

I appreciated the camaraderie both on and off the job, and saw the gratification and pride in their eyes of watching a patient make it after being written off for dead. I also thought that when they dropped off a patient at the emergency department, they had a little free time (boy, was I wrong) until the next call came in.

They were also on their own, responsible for life and death decisions, able to do things in the field that I could not dream of doing without a medical doctor physically present, even though a handful of the physicians we dealt with couldn't even find their way out of a paper bag without help from the nurses. On the other hand, the other Emergency Department nurses and I were responsible for patients that the rescue crews brought in hour after hour, day after day. At the time, our emergency department was the second busiest in the most heavily populated county in the State of Florida. Due to the overload, most patients were in our care from three to eight hours before being either discharged or admitted, based upon bed availability. In the meantime, more rescues or privately-operated ambulances would show up with additional patients, not to mention the walk-ins off the street. In time, I was convinced and sat for the firefighter entrance exam.

As a point of reference, after the sixth attempt to change the name from Metro-Dade to Miami-Dade County for a variety of reasons, the proponents of this politically-motivated push were finally successful in 1997. In order to avoid confusion, all further references to the county throughout these accounts will be as Miami-Dade.

When I first tested with Miami-Dade in 1974, there were four separate hiring lists: white male, black male, Hispanic male and female. My test scores were consistently in the high 90's, but this was the beginning of the era of political correctness. The objective was not necessarily to hire the best-qualified individual, but to make sure the demographics of the department reflected the community. But instead of recruitment efforts being concentrated on the military for those who had the drive and the self-discipline to become top-of-the-line firefighters and eventually officers who would lead the department, or looking at potential personnel from higher education institutions such as the local community colleges, the recruiting focused on shopping malls and high schools. What you get from that are individuals who look at the job as just that, a job; not a career. They want the good benefits and the allegedly great hours, but not the responsibilities and accountability that go with an occupation that deals with human beings physically and mentally at risk on a daily basis. Don't get me wrong; I personally have no problem with this mandate, as long as the best-qualified individuals from all ethnic groups and genders are chosen. I'm just setting the stage for why it took me so long to get on the department.

For several years, I applied to almost every fire department in Miami-Dade, Broward and Palm Beach, the three largest counties in South Florida. In some cases, I was able to take a written test, but most municipalities required a local address or never called me back. I continued to take the Miami-Dade test as well on an annual basis, but never getting a return call. I was close to calling it quits and seriously looked at making nursing my lifelong career. After a decade of taking the Miami-Dade and other tests, my best friend who was hired several years earlier called me and said, "Get your butt down to personnel. They may be hiring paramedics this year!"

This was the first year that those in power decided that it might be beneficial (not to mention cost-effective) to hire personnel who were already certified. They added a fifth hiring list for paramedics and I finally had the job I had tried to get for ten years. I was so happy to have been hired; I said I didn't care where they sent me. I would, and could work with anyone, anywhere, anytime. That was short-lived.

"THE GOLF BALL CHALLENGE"

It's been almost four decades since I lined up in a pair of orange shorts and white V-necked t-shirt as a raw, albeit 32-year-old recruit for my first day of Fire College. Despite the many years that have passed, I distinctly remember certain events that stuck out. The first was almost losing the job before I really had it.

In the early 80s, one of the components of the physical agility test to become a recruit was the golf ball test. This test consisted of the applicant standing erect with both feet together, as if at attention. He or she was then directed to reach down with his or her right hand to pick up the first of three golf balls placed next to, but outside the left foot, one at a time without bending the knees. The applicant would then transfer the golf ball to the left hand and place it on the ground outside the right foot. The process would then be repeated until all three golf balls were repositioned.

Now, we have been taught that in order to avoid back injuries when you bend and lift, you should spread your feet apart to give your body a wide base of support. You should also bend at the knees, not at the waist, and not to twist your back while bending to reach the object. The exercise component we were required to perform completely ignored all of these principles.

As it was, three other candidates and I were unable to complete the test since we couldn't reach the golf balls without bending our knees. According to testing regulations, that disqualified us and our careers were over before they had begun. Luckily, one of the Lieutenants assigned to recruit training stepped in saying the test was unsafe and made no sense. Using much more descriptive language sprinkled with profanities, he reiterated that using the standard of bending the knees and keeping the back straight as the only approved technique for lifting could expose the county to legal action.

The other training officers agreed with him and stopped the agility test. They apparently discussed it with the Captain in charge until the decision was made to remove the golf ball module from the testing process. We were reinstated and accepted into Fire College.

"THE 50-FOOT LADDER RAISE"

Once we made it to recruit training, one of the required performance measures was to complete a 50-foot Bangor ladder raise. Large wooden single section ladders were generally too heavy, and wooden extension ladders had a tendency to break where the bed (bottom) and fly (upper) sections joined. Most of the Bangors (possibly named after Bangor Maine but never verified) had tormentor or stay poles attached that were used in raising and stabilizing it (Angulo, 2012). Stay poles in the fire service were held in place by firefighters holding onto ropes that were tied to the ladders, not fixed to the ground or to solid objects. In the real world, the purpose was to rescue people trapped on multiple floors of a building by setting the ladder approximately two feet away at a 90-degree angle, purportedly allowing victims to step out of a window and climb down the ladder to safety. Sure. How many people actually made it past the two-feet of space between the building and the ladder safely? Two feet doesn't sound like a lot unless you're elderly, have a disability or a fear of heights.

In fire colleges or fire academies, the purpose was more of a team building exercise. Normally, once the Bangor ladder was raised, each recruit would climb to the top, cross over the uppermost rung, and work their way down the other side. Instead of tormentors, ropes tied to the beams were held in place by other recruits positioned near the end of each guy line.

Out of the 34 people in my recruit class, 12 were female. This was significant as until that time, no Miami-Dade Fire Department recruit class had totaled more than four women, and the mandate from administration was to increase the number of females in the department to represent the demographics of the community.

During that particular team building exercise, the instructors had everyone go two at a time, which doubled the weight on the ladder. In order to adjust to the extra weight, they had two recruits on each guy line. When it was our turn, they rotated personnel but as luck would have it, we only had female recruits on the lines.

Research has shown that women generally have approximately half the upper body strength of men (Miller, et al., 1993) (please don't' shoot the messenger! I'm sure that has changed significantly especially in the fire service, but these were the findings at that time). This meant that each guy line had the approximate holding strength of one male firefighter but double the weight on each line. As the other recruit and I climbed the ladder and looked down, we swore that several of the smaller women were struggling to hold the lines taut. This had to be more perception than reality, but when you're 50 feet off the ground with nothing between you and the pavement, you tend to think more in terms as the glass being half-empty.

As we got to the top, we had to negotiate around each other over the uppermost rung that was probably no more than 24 inches wide. Anthropologist Edward T. Hall described four levels of social distancing that occurs (Hall, 1959). The two that come into play are personal distance, which is 18 inches to four feet. At this distance, he explained that this level usually occurs between family members or close friends.

The second more applicable, is called intimate distance, which is six to 18 inches. According to Hall, this distance often indicates a closer relationship or greater comfort between individuals and can occur during intimate contact such as hugging or touching.

Two big boys take up a lot of room. 50 feet above the ground without a net makes for intimate friends, at least for several minutes. We made it safely and got to the ground in record time.

Most (not all) of the recruits successfully completed all the written and physical requirements to earn the title of Florida State Certified Firefighter. Now the real work began.

PART II: OPERATIONS

"FIRST DAYS ON THE JOB"

My first assignments were all in the North end of the County. For those outside the fire service, you may hear the terms, fire station, station, firehouse, house, or even hall, depending on the area of the country. These terms are generally interchangeable. This assignment was a "CR" or a cycle relief position put into play to avoid having personnel work in excess of 80 hours in a bi-weekly period and not go into overtime mode. Some departments call it a CR Day, and others a Kelly Day, named after Edward J. Kelly, Mayor of Chicago from 1933 to 1947, who lobbied for legislation in 1939 to give firefighters an extra day off.

There was nothing extraordinarily good or bad about this area of the County. Those three stations at the time were more or less middle-of-the-road as far as call volume, with more medical calls and less trauma due to a higher elderly population. Most of the firefighters did their jobs very well, but as I found out as my career progressed, the slower the house, the more complaining. One of these stations was the first that I had seen with three separate refrigerators and padlocks. It was also my first experience with the "me first" mentality.

One of the local condominium associations had donated a number of items to the station, including two toaster ovens. When one of the more pragmatic firefighters working at the station recommended giving the second toaster oven to another station that didn't have the benefit of an association or any other donors, one of the regulars actually said, "What if ours breaks? We need it as a backup." I realized much later that this was part of an entitlement mentality: the opposite to the brotherhood that I soon learned to appreciate.

Miami-Dade was and is no different from any large urban fire department. You have the vast majority of the organization who go to work, do their jobs well and hope to make it home safely. You also have the two extremes. The 10 to 15 percent who volunteer for every job and assignment, go to every class to improve themselves professionally, and are always the first in line when something needs to be done or someone needs help. This occurs outside of influential senior officers or mentors within the service, and includes signing up for didactic courses, taking hands-on training, and attending conferences and seminars to make them more proficient and gain valuable subject matter experience. You frequently see the same faces in many of those classes and training opportunities, month after month, and year after year.

At the other end of the spectrum is the two to five percent of the department who do everything they can to get out of actually doing the job for which they were hired. These are the people who never should have been hired in the first place, take every sick hour they have on the books, may end up on restricted duty, take an early out through disability, or worse, get someone injured or killed through their inability to effectively function as a firefighter. They're the ones who call in sick when a company, battalion, or division drill is scheduled, and the first to file a grievance when new or additional training is implemented.

Negligible as they may seem, they can become a glaring issue in the eyes of the public. Again, I have no problem with firefighters who have done their time in the field and prefer to work at a slower house as long as they continue to maintain their skills. It's those who sign up and find out firefighting is not for them. Instead of admitting that the job can, and will be dangerous, and that they are simply taking a position away from thousands of qualified people apply for annually, they milk the system by becoming an overpaid clerk.

Some get out of operations within a year or two of being hired by means of an "injury" or finding and filling a special assignment outside of operations. The worst part is that they continue to call themselves "firefighter." No organization is immune from this: if someone says those people don't exist in their agency; they're only kidding themselves.

The remaining percentage are the ones who usually go with the flow. If the Officer-in-Charge (OIC) is one that wants to train all day, most will have no problem with it. On the other hand, if the OIC says, today will be a down day and we'll take it easy, he or she probably won't get much of an argument. However, the goal is, and should be to refocus effort on the upper 10 to 15 percent of that group and mold them into eventual leaders in the fire service. It isn't easy, and doesn't always work, but the effort is well worth it when you see one or more several years later as an officer mentoring a new group of recruits. Training doesn't end when a recruit's probationary period ends: it's only the beginning and continues throughout one's career.

"YOU LEARN FROM THE GOOD AND BAD"

During my first few months, I was assigned to three of the most dissimilar officers I've seen in my career. Thankfully, they were truly the exception to the rule and nothing like others I worked for, with, or supervised throughout my time in the fire service. Whether you realize it or not, you are influenced by your officers, your peers, and your subordinates both good and bad. The influence of the inferior or substandard officer comes by remembering attitudes or problems associated with those individuals and promising to yourself that if you ever are promoted, you'll never be like them.

Without naming names, I had one officer who was eventually fired for allegedly not submitting run reports on every call. If true, failure to document as many as 200 reports by this individual could have resulted in a tremendous liability for the department had one or more of those calls gone to court. The main reason he was able to hide his shortcomings was that this took place years before computers were commonplace in the workforce, and each report was hand-written and carbon copied, not saved electronically.

The second officer was a real piece of work; his day revolved around what he wanted to do, where he could eat for free or where we received a discounted rate, what errands he was going to run, and whether he would get to take a nap. He wouldn't be in on dinner with the crews but would wait until dinner was over and order his crew to go by one of the hospitals only so that he could eat at no cost in their cafeterias. Running calls never came into play. He was a pleasant individual, but most of the fire service and the local emergency department staffs had little or no respect for him. However, as the ranking officer, they tolerated him as long as he did no harm and didn't violate policies.

Everything happens for a reason, and payback is a bitch so they say. Several years later, this individual was caught stealing pens from a local grocery store. When management confronted him, they offered him the opportunity to put the pens back and never to return to their store. Stupidly, he refused the offer and denied stealing the pens. A police report was made, and eventually this moron was forced to resign, all over a case of kleptomania. What made it worse was that he happened to pick the only major food chain where multiple crews shopped, tarnishing our reputations to the point that something had to be done.

This all occurred a few years after I was promoted to Lieutenant and working at Rescue 7. A few shifts after the incident, I told my crew we were going shopping for dinner at the same store where the incident occurred. They asked if we could go elsewhere as they were more than a little nervous about the possible reaction of store personnel when we walked in. I told them we had to confront the issue head-on or we would forever be branded as thieves.

As soon as we pulled up in the rescue, the security guards saw us and actually began to follow us as we walked in. The tension was palpable, and it felt like a hundred pair of eyes were staring at us. I approached one of the guards and asked to see the manager. As he came out of his office, you could see the disdain on his face and the invisible shield around him immediately went up. I introduced myself and apologized on behalf of my crew, my department, and the County. I told him that the officer stealing from his store was not representative of our department or fire rescue and deserved everything he got if not more. As I went on to apologize several more times and thank him and his personnel for what they did every day, the look on his face changed from anger and contempt as he realized I, and others wearing the uniform were not like the individual who stole from his store. When we left, we contacted the neighboring firehouses to let them know what occurred, and that they could return to the store with their heads held high.

The third officer was amicable, but not a real go-getter. I was a probationary firefighter assigned to his unit and he decided that it was important that I learn how to call in reports, especially after midnight. Therefore, on the nights when we ran three, four, or five calls after midnight, I had to struggle through figuring out how to fill out reports and call them in to the dispatcher while this officer went to sleep. A real leader! Probies have enough to worry about without completing reports that are clearly an officer's responsibilities. I've been told that this was standard practice in the service, but that still didn't make it right. Another lesson learned that would make me a better officer when I got the opportunity.

"COLLECTING FOR THE MDA"

My career was over almost as soon as it started. Each year since 1954, members of the International Association of Firefighters (IAFF) across the United States and Canada collect donations for the Muscular Dystrophy Association. We were no different. I was honored to be associated with such a worthy cause, and when our crews went out to collect during Labor Day weekend, I did it with pride and enthusiasm.

One of the many kids who benefitted from MDA with personnel from multiple South Florida Fire Departments. (I'm second from the right, back row).

We set up shop at an extremely busy intersection; the general rule back then was for at least one firefighter to be at each of the four corners. We were out there for about an hour or so on a Sunday afternoon and I had walked past a line of about 15 cars, collecting from about one-third of them. When the light changed, traffic moved forward and I turned to walk back to the intersection to start the whole process over again. Somehow, I felt, rather than heard a car coming up from behind. I glanced to my right and saw a heavy, older sedan fly by me no more than 10 feet away. I would have sworn that there was no driver and the car was moving under its own power. If it had hit me, there was no question that I would have been badly injured or killed. Everything seemed to slow down, but I know that was only an illusion. It was as if I was watching from further away as the car passed me and careened into several parked cars in a pizza restaurant parking lot.

Almost as soon as the crash occurred, everything snapped back to reality. I ran over to the crash site, as did the rest of the firefighters who had been collecting. On the floorboard of the car was the driver, drunk out of his mind, but so relaxed he had passed out and slid off the seat before the crash. Luckily, no bystander was injured and not surprisingly, neither was the driver. I say that because the rule is "bad guys don't die, and drunks don't get hurt in accidents." Our law enforcement brethren took the individual into custody and we went back to collecting for the MDA.

"THE MOON MAN"

I spent my first three months working out of these stations for a Battalion Captain who had a penchant for staying out after midnight. His crews nicknamed him the "Moon Man" as he ostensibly traveled by the light of the moon. It was said that he had problems sleeping, stayed up most of the night, and would just drive around even if he weren't on a call. I heard that he considered every firefighter's accrued time to be his own and would take it personally if someone called in sick. As a probationary firefighter, I had no intentions of calling in sick unless my leg was cut off. However, as luck would have it, I came down with a virus that was making the rounds and it kicked my butt. Halfway through my shift, I became febrile and started sweating. This continued for a couple of hours until one of the veteran firefighters noticed I was pale and soaked with sweat. "Rookie, if you're sick, get out of my station before you infect everybody else." I told him that I was on probation and afraid to take any time off. He told me that if you're sick, you're sick (typical firefighter, come right to the point, no BS), and not to come back until you're well again. Since I had heard about this Captain's feelings toward sick time use, I hung on until shift change at 07:00 hours. I spent the next two days off in bed and felt no better when I got up to go to work for the next shift and I knew I couldn't make it. I called in sick, stayed in bed for another day and a half, and went to work on the following duty day.

Predictably, the Captain called me into his office and harangued me at length about taking a sick day. He lectured me about my responsibilities as a probationary firefighter, saying that my career could be short-lived if I abused sick leave (all this over one sick day!). He then told me that in one week, I would be transferred indefinitely to Battalion 5 to ride the Stations 2, 7, and 30 rescue CR cycle. I realized I was being punished (or so I thought at the time), packed my gear and waited to head south, so to speak.

The stories about Battalion 5 were endless. For the next week, multiple firefighters and officers said they did their time there and would never go back. What I later discovered was what they considered doing their time usually meant one or two shifts, or heaven forbid, a full bid period of six months. Many veteran firefighters refused to take promotional exams for fear that they would be assigned to ride in Battalion 5.

A good friend, Dr. Dan Whu, a retired Battalion Chief and practicing physician, told me years later that everything happens for a reason. I didn't believe it at the time, but as time went on, I realized he was dead right. In hindsight, I also realize that this reassignment would be the defining moment of my career.

PART III: WELCOME TO BATTALION 5

"THE DEUCE"

What a change! Year in and year out, Rescue 2 remained one of the five or six busiest rescue units in the country: not the county, but the entire country. The aerial also ranked in the top 10 annually and was actually a more active unit. Squrt 2 (trademark name for an aerial) was the busiest aerial truck on the North America continent in 1999 and 2000. Station 7 was right behind them: Engine 7 saw more structure fires than any other engine in Miami-Dade County, which translated to one of the busiest in the Southeast United States, and Rescue 7 was in the top five busiest units, including all suppression units for fires in the County. Station 2 had one rescue, one Squrt, and one Battalion Captain (later with reorganization upgraded to Battalion Chief), averaging close to 13,000 calls per year for mostly the rescue and Squrt. Stations 7 and 30 weren't far behind.

Station 2 is commonly thought to be in the area referred to as Liberty City, but is actually in Model City, the correct historical name for the area. When I arrived at the station a half-hour early to try to make a good impression, three or four of the firefighters were already there, including the Battalion Chief and the Rescue Lieutenant. They were already putting their gear on the apparatus (fire department-speak for the trucks). This shocked me to no end because during my time in the other stations many of the personnel came in just before shift change at 07:00 hours (unflatteringly referred to as minutemen). Typically, many who arrived early did not get on his or her assigned truck until just before or at shift change. Frequently the off-going firefighter would have to run a late call, and not get back to the station until 07:30 or 08:00 hours. This could be tough if you've got other responsibilities such as taking your kids to school or going to a second job.

This didn't go over well in Battalion 5 where Stations 2, 7, and 30 were located. The rules were simple; you were expected to be ready to run a call at 07:00 hours, not start getting on the truck. You came to work with the expectations that you would be awake for your 24-hour tour of duty, and if you got any sleep, well that was a bonus. Work hard, play hard was the unwritten motto.

Everybody got along great, and the Battalion Captain sent those who didn't down the road. One of the things that impressed me the most about working at the stations was that it was an extremely diverse group of people: White, Black, Puerto Ricans, Cubans, Christian, Jews, men and women. You didn't see different ethnic groups going off by themselves or not interacting as friends. As I found out, I would come to consider these firefighters as family, and many of them have remained my friends for life.

Several months later, we returned from a call and the Battalion Captain, Drennon Barton, told me that the same Captain who reamed me for being sick wanted to talk to me and bring me back to his battalion. Captain Barton advised me to ask for permission to stay in Battalion 5 and that he would work to keep me. When I spoke to the other Captain, I was respectful and did exactly as I was directed. He went ballistic, screaming and cursing at me. I said nothing and took the brunt of his vitriol. When he hung up, Captain Barton laughed and said to expect to bounce around the County for a few months but he'd eventually bring me back.

True to form, the next shift I was reassigned to one of the south end stations, and for several shifts, had the opportunity to visit the far reaches of Miami-Dade County. To rub it in, the crews from Station 2 would call to tell me they just had a warehouse fire, multiple shooting, or another major incident, laugh and hang up. After several weeks that seemed like months, I was able to go back to Battalion 5 where I would spend the next 20 years.

"TOURISTS WELCOME"

I didn't have to wait long to see why the area had a reputation for being busy. One of the first calls we responded to was a head-on accident involving a family from Virginia and three purse-snatchers in a stolen vehicle. The purse-snatchers were headed eastbound at over 80 mph and struck the car with the tourists almost directly head-on. When we arrived, the cars had been thrown approximately 250 feet apart from the force of the impact.

My Lieutenant, Duke Adkinson, told me to check the car that was furthest away, while he and the other firefighter, Gene Kemp, ran to the first vehicle where three victims could be seen hanging out of the car (more about Duke and Gene later).

I have to expound on a couple of points. All of this occurred during a four-to-five-minute time span: we arrived on the scene within three minutes of receiving the call and were totally on our own. Our Squrt crew was on another call, and the next available suppression unit was coming from several miles away. Captain Barton arrived seconds after we did and immediately ordered mutual aid from the City of Miami. As I said before, my officer and the driver found the first car on its side with the three victims stacked on top of each other, hanging out the open window. The two on top were dead, but the one pinned underneath was still alive.

Meanwhile, I had arrived at the other vehicle. The driver was obviously dead, as the force of the impact had driven the engine through the both the firewall and his body killing him instantly and pinning the passenger in the back seat directly behind the driver. Two other passengers were thrown from the car and appeared to be unconscious. Well, this is what I asked for: being responsible for life and death decisions, able to do things without being told how or when. A little more than I expected, no, a lot more, but here I was.

One of our off-duty firefighters had been driving by and asked how he could help. I told him to check on the people who were ejected from the car while I examined the passenger in the back seat. He was unresponsive with multiple obvious open fractures from head to toe. While I immobilized his cervical spine and started an intravenous line, my partners were experiencing a little more than they expected.

While they were in the car trying to get to the lone remaining survivor, the car caught fire. Luckily, Squrt 2 had cleared the previous scene, arrived and extinguished the fire before our guys were injured. Several more rescues and suppression units from both Miami-Dade County and the cities of Miami and Hialeah began to arrive. I turned over the three patients I had to other units and went back to assist my crew.

At that point, the police told us that our patient was one of the "bad guys." The officers wanted us to do everything we could to ensure he survived to receive his due process, was prosecuted, and put away for many years. Somehow, he survived the accident and one of the rescues transported him to the Trauma Center. A few weeks later, one of the cops told us that since prosecutors were unable to place him behind the wheel of the stolen car, and no items from the stolen purses were found on him, they were powerless to charge him with a felony offense.

An innocent person on vacation dies with the rest of his family severely injured, and this piece of garbage that was responsible walked away scot-free. The three of us agreed that regardless of the rules, we would never put the extra effort in to save a bad guy again.

"SIZE MATTERS"

After going to Battalion 5, I was fortunate in being assigned to some of the best officers anyone could ask for. Everyone had vastly different personalities but were alike in the respect that they were there to do the job to the best of their ability. Who and what I became in the fire service was based upon what I learned from each and every one of them, firefighters included. On one of those crews, I had the opportunity to work with Captain Hal Sears, and Gene Kemp who I mentioned earlier. Both of them became good friends, and I had known Hal from my days working at Hialeah Hospital. Gene and I eventually became roommates (that's not another story, that's a book by itself!). At the time I rode with them, Hal was a former All-American college linebacker about 5' 10 and 230 lbs., and one of the strongest human beings I have ever seen. I was 6' 2" and 220, Gene was 6' 6" and 250, and all three of us were in good shape at the time.

The reason I bring this up is a call we ran late one night. I don't remember why we were called, but I do remember that it was in the Liberty Square projects, one of the areas in our response zone in the 1980's where we couldn't leave the rescue truck to take care of a patient without locking all the compartments. If we didn't, the truck would be cleaned out or gone when we got back. It wouldn't be the first time one of our trucks was stolen.

Most of the time, you knew you were being sized up by the gang-bangers but our size alone prevented most problems. On this particular call, we came up on a third-floor apartment with the door slightly open, music blaring, and the aroma of marijuana permeating the air. Hal knocked on the door, and there was no answer. He pushed it open a little further, and five or six older teens who thought they were bad asses gave him a look as he walked in. Immediately afterward, I stepped through the doorway, and finally, Gene moved forward and blocked the doorway with his huge frame. He bent down for additional effect and stepped inside. The guys turned their music off and suddenly became quiet and a little more attentive and respectful. We went about our business and took care of the patient. It turned out to be the niece of one of the gangbangers and her mother had called. It is funny how at times size does mean everything.

"PROTECTING THE JEWELS"

On another call, the three of us responded to a woman apparently unresponsive on the ground. When we arrived, it was obvious that the patient was feigning unconsciousness. It's relatively easy to determine if someone is faking it: if you hold their hand above their head and let it go, they may inadvertently smack themselves in the face, but the second time you let it go, their hand will conveniently fall to the side. There are other methods but that one's tried and true. She was a patient in a nearby halfway house for mental illness, had taken an unauthorized walk, and knew she had violated the house rules. Gene and Hal went over to the patient to talk to her and try to elicit some information. For a big guy, Hal was very soft-spoken and rarely raised his voice. He was always a gentleman and regardless of the situation, was respectful to both patients and families. As he leaned over to talk to her in a low voice to try to get her to sit up, she suddenly wrapped her arms around his thigh, holding on in a death grip. Hal carefully and slowly moved his hands down to just above hers to protect his more sensitive parts. Gene and I looked at each other and sprang into action. I grabbed the clipboard while Gene took Hal's pen from him and we backed off, moving back to the safety of the rescue to watch the show. Hal called us a few choice names under his breath and for over 45 minutes, tried to coax this young lady into releasing his leg. Eventually, she did relax her grip and Hal was able to escape with all body parts intact.

Hal and Gene before the excitement begins!

"HE REALLY HAD TO GO"

Aside from this author, many firefighters are mechanically inclined. They can take anything apart, diagnose the problem and put it back together without any problems. Many others, including myself have Type "A" personalities (traits include need to win at everything, work-obsessed, and impatient). To this end, several of the Rescues had unofficial mascots ranging from Teenage Mutant Ninja Turtles to Gumby to various Disney characters. We took it a step further by hooking up a rubber Mickey Mouse firefighter to the front of the hood on Rescue 2 and used rubber tubing to attach it to the windshield washer. Mickey was dressed in bunker gear and a helmet and was holding a hose; whenever we pushed the washer button, we were able to squirt water about 15 feet through his hose line.

Here's Mickey!

It was a good joke or so we thought; especially when we convinced someone to check out our new mascot at close range and were hit with a spray of water. At one point, we were actually able to put out a small fire in a trash barrel. It was fun until Gene squirted a nurse while she was crossing the street in front of one of the hospitals. She apparently didn't appreciate our sense of humor and made a complaint. From that point on, all mascots were required to be non-functional and were eventually removed from the trucks.

If you look closely, you can see the stream from the Mickey mascot reaching the burn barrel.

"A DANGEROUS PROFESSION"

1995-New Year's Day: It was mid-afternoon when the dispatcher's voice radio crackled over the radio, "possible church fire". Given that it was a Sunday, the odds were good that the church was still occupied following the morning services. We were working on Rescue 7, one of central division's busier units and were clearing from another call out of our territory. Engine 7, the first-due suppression unit from West Little River, Squrt 2 from Liberty City, and Rescue 26 from Opa-Locka had already arrived. The remainder of the second alarm assignment was still in route.

Engine 7 was the first unit on-scene. Almost as soon as they arrived, they were surrounded by frantic members of the congregation with conflicting reports as to whether anyone was still inside. The officer assumed command and gave a quick size-up: a two-story CBS (concrete-block structure) church with light smoke showing from the second-floor northside of the structure, possible victims still inside. He decided to make a quick attack and began a search for trapped parishioners and the source of the fire. Squrt 2 hooked up to a hydrant, laid a backup line, and assisted in the search. Since Rescue 26's crew was already setting up as medical sector, we went directly to the Battalion Chief for an assignment.

Witnesses told him that the pastor was missing and they thought he had gone back inside the church to make sure everyone else was out. The Chief directed us to search the second floor at the south end, as the first floor had been evacuated and was almost cleared. Engine 7's crew had made their way to the second floor at the north end looking for the seat of the fire. If he was inside, the missing pastor would most likely be at our end of the church.

We entered the building via the southeast stairwell, taking for granted that it would open into the east side of the church. The last time this church was inspected was almost one year earlier, and there had been significant additions and changes since then that were not identified on the pre-fire plans. When we opened the door at the top of the stairwell, we found ourselves on the west side of the church. Regardless of where we were, we had a job to do, so we began our search in the vestries or side rooms.

Visibility was relatively good, but there was some light-colored smoke coming out of the eaves, a sign that the fire was not yet out. When we started our search in the first vestry, I reached above, touched the dropped ceiling to check for heat, and found it cool to the touch. This is normally an indication that there's no fire overhead. What we did find was that an opaque protective film was installed on both the inside and outside of the exterior windows. This film also hid the security bars that had been installed since the last inspection; not just on the outside as is usually done, but on the inside of each window as well, making the bars virtually invisible from the outside.

We continued our search, room by room, but as we began to exit the fifth vestry, the building erupted in thick black smoke pouring from the now collapsing false ceilings. Visibility instantly dropped to zero, and the heat from the fire drove us back into the room. We heard a loud roar and a crash, which we later discovered to be a large commercial fan no longer used but still attached to the original ceiling above the two recent additions. At a walkthrough, a day or so after the fire, we realized that we would have been severely injured or killed had the 200-lb. fan fallen on us. The fire's point of origin was later determined to be an electrical box at the north end of the church, directly below the area where Engine 7 was searching. Through the channel created above the first false ceiling, it raced to the south end of the building without detection.

We were in the nearest room to the left.

When we realized we were cut off from our original entry point and trapped on three sides by quickly worsening fire conditions, we had to work quickly. Our only way out at this point was through the second-story window: I advised the Battalion Chief of our situation but was unable to give him our exact location due to the lack of visibility which had been reduced to the point that we could barely see our gloves in front of our masks. We started to tear the protective film off the window while at the same time, prying the security bars out of the masonry. Time was of the essence: the fire was moving fast and had already vented, and the other crews had difficulty finding us due to the unusual configuration of the stairwells.

It took a few minutes just to rip the film off the windows to get to the security bars. Using a halligan and all our strength, we pried the bars out of the concrete. The next step was to break the windows and tear off the outer layer of film holding the remaining broken glass in place.

The fifth window from the right (partially obscured by the Aerial) was our escape route.

We had been in the room for several minutes and breathing hard: we were running low on air and the fire was now just outside the doorway.

We finally broke through the outer protective film, pushing the shards of glass out and away from us. Using our nylon webbing, we lowered my crew, Joe Sollecito first, then Bobby Flintroy to the parapet about four feet below. As I was tying my webbing to the discarded security bars to lower myself out, a firefighter from Rescue 26 looked up and realized they had to move fast. An extension ladder was raised to our position, allowing us to escape from the fire with minutes to spare.

For months, the second-guessing and rumors accused us of free-lancing and going in without a set of irons (a halligan and axe) which wasn't true. It was amazing how many of our own people thought we took it upon ourselves to jump the call and make entry without a mission. We were ordered to search for the pastor who by the way, was not on the scene and found safely at home a few hours later. We later also discovered was that there was not one, but two false ceilings installed, concealing the fire. The installation most likely took place without obtaining a permit to save on expenses. It could have been much worse but that day luck was with us.

"ANKLE BITERS"

From the beginnings of Emergency Medical Services in the 1960s until well into the 1990s, many Fire Departments providing pre-hospital care used fishing tackle boxes as the containers of choice to carry medical supplies from the trucks to the patients. These large orange and white boxes weighed about 12 pounds when empty, but more than doubled in weight when full. At MDFR, one box was labeled the Med Box, and a second was the Trauma Box. Regardless of the call, both boxes were brought in on almost every call. In addition, we carried a Motorola 12-Watt Apcor UHF telemetry radio (Revolvy, 2014) that weighed about 25 lbs., a Lifepak that weighed in at a hefty 45 lbs., and an oxygen cylinder about 10 lbs. including regulator, tubing and masks. In all, we had to carry 120 lbs. of equipment in on every call. As the most seniority-challenged paramedic, one of my jobs was to carry the Med Box, the Trauma Box, and the oxygen.

On this particular call, we had to make entry into a side yard of a duplex. The gate was open but when we walked inside, five or six Chihuahuas came sprinting out of a hole they had dug under the building. They were going crazy and doing their best to bite us. It was more annoying than dangerous as they were biting into our steel toe, steel heel, high top leather boots. I kept trying to move out of their way but they wouldn't give up and continued to bite at my boots. I finally had enough and when one got close, I simply let go of one of the boxes that fell squarely on the dog. It looked like a cartoon as the dog disappeared except for all four legs splayed out to the sides in the soft sand. The yapping immediately stopped and the other dogs turned tail and ran. I picked up the box that I had dropped, and the Chihuahua that was briefly pinned jumped up and ran as if his life depended on it, never looking back. When we cleared the call, we could see the dogs under the duplex, but they had no intentions of blocking our way back to the truck.

"HUMAN AIR HOCKEY"

Returning from a call one day, I was riding as the third medic on
Rescue 7. In the old trucks, the number-three medic faced backwards
in a fixed jump seat designed to be at the head of any patient who
was being transported. From this vantage point, I could see out both
the side and back windows. I noticed a kid in his 20's on a motor
scooter coming up fast, or at least as fast a 50cc engine could take him.
Dressed in long pants, a shirt and sneakers, and without a helmet, he
passed us on the right at doing about 45 mph. He either clipped some
debris in the road or oversteered as his front wheel began to wobble
back forth, first slightly, then violently. I yelled to my Lieutenant,
"Three o'clock; this guy's going to lose it!"

Suddenly, the front of the scooter went out from under him. He
went over the handlebars and somehow landed right on his butt on
the asphalt street, facing forward in a sitting position. Nevertheless, he
kept going: we watched him pass us on the right, at least 10 mph faster
than our truck. It's one of those OMG moments when you know
it's not going to end well. He hit the curb with both feet extended;
stopped suddenly and was tossed into the air like a rag doll. He was
thrown about 40 feet into some bushes and disappeared. By now, we
had pulled to a stop, jumped out, and run to the scene. We expected
to find either a fatality or at best, a critically injured patient. By the
time we reached him, he was standing up, picking branches and leaves

out of his hair. He insisted he was okay, but when we started to examine him, we saw that the seat of his pants had burned completely through, down to his underwear. Incredibly, with the exception of a few abrasions, he had no injuries. He fell off his scooter at over 35 mph, impacted a concrete curb with his feet, and flew for almost 40 feet without a helmet. He had no fractures, no lacerations, nothing except losing the seat of his pants and his dignity.

What a ride!

He didn't want to go to the hospital but we insisted, and after 10 minutes or so agreed to go. When we checked back with the hospital staff a few hours later, they said the x-rays were negative and he had been discharged. You could tell they were skeptical about the whole incident but we knew what we had seen. After the photo was printed (long before cellphones), I brought it to them and they couldn't believe that he was able to walk away from the accident. When it's your time to go, it's your time to go. If not, you get to live to do something stupid another day.

"FIREHOUSE HUMOR"

One great thing about the fire service are the practical jokes. Even more so in the busier houses; if they like you, they'll play with you, make fun of you, deride you, and play practical jokes on you every chance they get. There is no malicious intent, just the chance to let off steam in a protected environment, so to speak. This is discussed at length in several subsequent chapters. One of those jokes involved a simple, yet effective way of annoying your brothers and sister firefighters without doing any damage.

When you sprinkled a small amount (key word being "small"), of grated parmesan cheese inside someone's pillowcase onto their pillow, it quickly reminded you of the odor of a pair of socks that had been worn for several consecutive days. After submitting one of our brother firefighters to this indignity every shift for about a week, the top to a large container of grated cheese came off during one of the shakeouts, spilling the entire 16-ounce contents onto the pillow. Grated cheese is not meant to be returned to its container once removed, nor is it intended to be exposed to pillow fibers and expected to be separated again. It's easier to remove Velcro using your feet. The pillow stunk like cheese and we had to buy a replacement before he tried to hit the sack that shift.

Another practical joke that was perpetrated on the unsuspecting was to unscrew the communal showerheads and put bouillon cubes inside. Bouillon cubes are compressed, flavor-concentrated cube of dehydrated meat, fish, poultry or vegetable stock. Once mixed with hot water, the mixture becomes broth.

For some reason, olfactory cognition, or the ability to recognize smells in many people becomes muted or the smell of broth in that particular environment just doesn't register. It's similar to not having showered for a while; you can't smell your own body odor, but you can bet that everyone else can. After a hot shower of beef or chicken broth rubbed into your skin, you dress and go about your merry way, unaware that you smell like beef stew or chicken tacos. One of the guys swears he was followed by a clowder (that's what they're called) of cats after a bouillon shower.

Another tried and true method of tormenting your colleagues is to have them spray themselves with water when they open the kitchen faucet. Transparent tape is used to keep the handle of the spray hose attachment in an open position and aimed at where the unsuspecting victim will probably stand. When the faucet is opened, the diverter valve opens and the water comes out of the sprayer instead of the faucet.

Alan Cominsky, one of my all-time favorite rookies who rose through the ranks to become Chief of the Department was assigned to Firehouse 7 when we decided to victimize our next target. We told Alan that if he taped the sprayer, no one would know that he had done it. He was worried that he since he was on probation, he'd get in trouble or possibly lose his job. He was a go-getter, all of his supervisors liked him, and he was safe with being in on the joke. He didn't know that the joke was actually on him.

We promised that absolutely no one would ever know he had done it. Reluctantly, he put the tape on and we waited. Eventually,

Manny Morales from Engine 7 came into the kitchen: Manny was one of the best damn firefighters I had ever worked with and I'll have more on him later. In physical terms, Manny wasn't a big man, but he had an intimidating presence around those who didn't know him. Of course, he turned the water on and the spray soaked his shirt. He turned and yelled, "Who did this?" Almost as one, we pointed to Mr. Cominsky. His mouth dropped open and there was fear in his eyes. Before anyone had a chance to say anything, he bolted for the door. We ran after him but he was already headed south down 22nd Avenue, the main thoroughfare in front of the firehouse. It took us more than a few minutes to convince him that he wasn't going to lose his job.

Last but certainly not least, I mentioned earlier that the old Firehouse 7 was one of the smallest stations in the County. It had a combined kitchen/dining/living/office area with probably no more than 800 square feet. The rescue and engine dorms had just enough room for seven people with the bunks, old metal lockers for 21 firefighters (three shifts worth), and space enough to get by only if you turned sideways. It was a rented space in a storefront with the other tenant being a paint and body shop. The rescue dorm abutted the paint and body shop: every time they turned on the paint sprayers or generators next door, the walls would shake. There was only one small bathroom with a toilet and shower, tough for seven adults to share, especially after a fire or two that day. The bathroom and plumbing were also 25 years old. Once in a while when the toilet backed up, feces would come up through the shower stall, a distinctively unpleasant surprise for the occupant. Somehow, at times the hot water would also mysteriously be turned off and a stream of profanities would emanate from the shower stall.

Nymphs at play.

Everyone knows that South Florida is the retirement home for elderly northeasterners, but over the years, we have become the vacation destination and eventual permanent home for invasive plant and animal species that have overrun the area. More than 500 species of all fish, reptiles, birds, and mammals in Florida are non-native (FWC, 2018), and many of those are in South Florida. Our unwanted guests include the walking catfish which can breathe air and pull themselves along the ground with their pectoral fins (FWC, 1999); giant African land snails up to eight inches long that can transmit meningitis (United States Department of Agriculture, 2016); and of course, the Burmese python. One captured in the Everglades measured almost 19 feet long, and another actually tried to swallow an alligator and died in the process.

Now that we've gotten the fun facts out of the way, let's talk about the domestic Eastern Lubber Grasshopper, which grows up to three and one-half inches long and is indigenous to the Southeastern United States. These grasshoppers love weed-covered fields and vegetation, are brightly colored, toxic, and emit a bubbling froth and loud hissing sound from their thoraxes when threatened. Sometimes they come in waves and hundreds are found in urban areas munching on anything green. Nymphs, or their young are almost completely black with a bright yellow, orange, or red dorsal stripe. They are slower with a soft exoskeleton and easier to catch. When picked up by the dozens and deposited in a dark bathroom for the first unsuspecting victim, it provides the desired response.

One of the senior firefighters on Engine 7 was as regimented as they come. If his crew wasn't on a run, he would try to eat a can of tuna every day around the same time. The European Food Council (it really exists) identifies that the time for human digestion depends on the consistency, temperature and particle size of food as well as the amount of liquid we drink, etc., etc. In layman's terms, it means that if you eat, you have to go. We knew that after a certain time frame, he'd have to use the bathroom, which he did. As many of us would, we'd focus on the job at hand, not the aesthetics of the environment.

Once seated, his three dozen or so roommates started to crawl down the wall to join him on the throne. This didn't "sit" well with him and we heard yelling from the commode, followed by an early exit.

"A TIME FOR EVERY SEASON"

It's been said that everything happens for a reason. If it's your time to go, then it's destined to occur: most of us never expect that time to be on the horizon. When you are in your car with your family, drive the speed limit and obey all traffic laws, you don't expect anything to happen, especially an unsecured piece of steel that falls off a moving truck at 40 mph. In this case, the steel bounced several times and according to witnesses, actually went completely over another car. The piece of steel could have gone to the left or to the right: instead, its trajectory took it directly toward this family's car, piercing the windshield where one of the sons was sitting between his dad and his brother. The son was hit in the left side of his head just above the eyebrow, sustaining a major head injury. To make matters worse, the piece of metal was twisted: once it penetrated the windshield it struck the father, killing him instantly.

In a split-second, this family was destroyed and the responsible party drove off, never knowing that they were liable for someone's death. I can't begin to tell you how many times we ran on accidents that were caused by unsecured items that fell off vehicles such as furniture, iron reinforcing rods, mattresses, or even kitchen appliances. The other major causes were tires, car or truck parts post-accident, or construction-related items. Most of the fatalities and critical injuries were unnecessary and could have been easily avoided.

This happened far too often.

"DRINK RESPONSIBLY"

As I stated earlier, we kept a police scanner in our truck to get a jump on calls, whether they were in our territory or nearby. We heard a police chase involving a beer truck stolen at gunpoint and jumped the call as soon as we cleared the one we were on. By the time we arrived, the truck had been driven at a high rate of speed into a lake near a condominium. The police said the driver was still in the vehicle, so we donned our dive gear and went in for a search.

After the truck was towed out of the water.

When we entered the water, the truck had been partially submerged for 12-15 minutes and we thought we were in body recovery rather than rescue mode. The water was murky due to the silt that had been stirred up by the truck, and our visibility was less than one foot. My dive partner who I was tethered to pulled the line hard: I swam to where he was and realized he had found the individual who had stolen the truck. However, he was neither passive nor unconscious. He was kicking and fighting; apparently, he had stayed in an air pocket inside the back of the truck and had no intention of going to jail. The situation was dangerous for us, so we pulled away and surfaced. We told the cops that he was alive and fighting us. They said no problem, we can wait. After an additional 20 plus minutes, the perpetrator surfaced, stood on the hood of the truck and put his arms in the air, surrendering. Other than a severe case of pruney fingers due to his extended stay in the water, he was unhurt. After a quick exam, he was carted off to jail.

"IS THAT A BANANA IN YOUR PANTS?"

One of the main roads that divided the response zones of Stations 2 and 7 was 79th St. In the early 1980's, 79th St. on Friday and Saturday nights was the place to be for hundreds of people hanging out, drinking and partying to the deafening sounds of boom-boxes and 200-watt car speakers that could be heard one-half mile or more away. For the most part, it remained relatively peaceful with the occasional shooting, stabbing, or assault with whatever weapon was handy.

This was also a largely heterosexual crowd. However, there was a small section where individuals with alternative sexual lifestyles were accommodated. They were informally accepted by the community as long as they stayed within their invisible boundaries. Although the cost of transsexual surgery (also known as sex reassignment) was prohibitive in the 1980s and 1990s, especially in the lower socio-economic areas, some of those leaning in that direction would dress the part and add certain accoutrements (such as water balloons as breasts or tucking their genitals between their legs) to appear more feminine. In addition, many would work as prostitutes to get enough money for the surgery, specializing in oral sex with customers from outside the area. We in Fire Rescue were well aware due to the fact that our friends in law enforcement would joke about the large number of upstanding citizens, including attorneys, judges, politicians and other professionals from affluent areas who would come to the area for a quickie, not knowing their partner of the moment was of the same sex. Additionally, many were arrested as undercover police officers frequently set up stings in the area.

As it happened one Saturday night, one of the customers was conducting negotiations with one of the "working girls" for some oral gratification while both were in his car. Inevitably, things went south when the customer in the throes of passion reached under his paramour's skirt and grabbed a package bigger than his own. Apparently humiliated, he quickly changed his demeanor and pulled out a screwdriver stabbing the prostitute in the center of the chest. He pushed her/him out of his car and tried to flee but was caught by police officers after blowing through a red light about a block away.

The police called for Rescue and when we arrived, the victim was in the street, covered with blood and the perpetrator in custody. Protocols called for quickly exposing the wound, which we did; cutting the shirt open also allowed two large water balloons to fall out. As there is very little mercy in the mean streets of Miami, the crowd went wild, laughing derisively. As always, we remained professional, continued to treat the victim and transported him to the trauma center where he was pronounced dead.

"OUR BROTHERS
IN BROWN"

Miami-Dade Police Department officers have historically worn brown uniforms as opposed to the typical green for other County police departments, and the standard blue for officers working for municipalities. They pay an annual fine to the State of Florida for the right to do so. As I said earlier, we had an outstanding relationship with all law enforcement, but especially the police officers in the district. We always had their backs, and they always had ours. If we saw an officer on a call or a traffic stop, day or night, we would regularly pull over and wait until they cleared the scene, had backup, or waved us off.

They did the same for us and it was always greatly appreciated. We did have fun with them however. We would drop ammonia inhalants which were normally used to revive victims (no longer recommended but this was 30 plus years ago) into their air conditioning vents in their patrol cars so the smell would be nasty but not overpowering.

They returned the favor early one morning around 03:30 hours. A patrol car slowly passed us on the left; the officer waved, and we returned the greeting. As he unhurriedly shifted into our lane a few car lengths ahead, a second car moved up, riding flanking us. By the time we realized the lead car was slowing down and a third car had quickly pulled up behind us, we had no place to go and were forced to a stop. In the old rescues, there were no power windows; they had to be rolled up by hand and there was a small triangular vent window on each side of the cab. We knew we had to act fast, rolled the windows up as quickly as possible and locked all the doors, but were unable to lock the passenger side vent window before they reached us. One of the officers took advantage of the opportunity to discharge a dry chemical extinguisher that he carried in his unit. At the time, dry chemical extinguishers sprayed a very fine powder of either sodium bicarbonate (baking soda), potassium bicarbonate (nearly identical to baking soda), or mono-ammonium phosphate. These are designed to coat the fuel and smother a fire by displacing oxygen, making our decision to bail out of the truck that much easier. The contents will coat every possible surface, nook and cranny in a rescue truck, or on the personnel who happen to be inside.

We congratulated the cops on at long last getting back at us, but we all knew that the game was far from over and actually had been elevated to the next level. We returned to the firehouse and showered several times, then went to work cleaning the interior of the truck which took most of what was left of the shift.

I want to be very clear that the roughhousing and practical jokes that we played did not interfere with our ability to respond to calls, nor did it cost the citizens of Miami-Dade County a single penny. We would refill extinguishers out of pocket, replace any items we used, or in many cases upgraded the tools and equipment we used to protect the public through a kitty at the station specifically for these purposes, including buying a reciprocating saw and an air chisel. These practical jokes were and continue to be a way of allowing us to deal with the multitude of distress, grief, suffering, and misfortune encountered on almost a daily basis.

The Miami-Dade Police Department Northside District station fronted on a semi-residential neighborhood but was adjacent to a large flea market, multiple small businesses, and backed up against several large parking lots. The District grounds were fenced in, but parking for the officers as well as the area where they refueled was on the south side of the building, open to these parking areas and to 79th Street. This was a relatively busy road, but an opportune area to escape in multiple directions if you have just shot at cops. To protect the officers from this type of activity, multiple tractor-trailers were parked end to end next to the south end of their secured area.

We knew most of the officers on a first name basis, as well as the shifts they worked and when they would break to refuel. Having run dozens of calls at the District station, we were familiar with the building layout as well as the parking area and perimeter. One of the guys came up with a plan to shoot water balloons over the trailers at our law enforcement partners while they were refueling.

To that end, we decided to build a large slingshot made of surgical tubing that would give us the ability to shoot the distance necessary to hit our marks. Surgical tubing is made of latex and typically used to pump fluids in or out of patients during surgical procedures but can be used for a multitude of different contrivances. We used about six feet of three-sixteenth inch diameter tube in conjunction with an old surgical mask as an ammo pouch: this created a slingshot capable of hurling water balloons a hundred feet or so with relative accuracy.

An important point to remember: do not play with or perform practical jokes on those you know won't appreciate it, those you don't know very well, and those who may take offense to being the butt of the joke. Most importantly, do no harm to the individual, the agency, or the community. In other words, protect people, property and the environment.

Once every shift or so, depending if we had some down time after midnight, we'd drive to the rear of District 2's parking area and set up behind the trailers, blocking our view of the officers and their ability to see us except for a few inches between the trailers. Since this was still in our response zone, we would simply advise dispatch that we were '09', or in service. We'd monitor our radios and walk around the trailers to see if anyone we knew was in the back of the lot refueling. If we saw one of the officers we recognized, we'd quickly retreat to our original position. Two of us would hold the ends of the surgical tubing, while the third crewmember would load a pre-filled water balloon into the surgical mask and let fly. Sometimes they would land close enough for the officers to quickly look around and peer through the fence to see if anyone was there. We occasionally had a direct hit but were always close enough to let them know we were out there.

"LEADERSHIP"

We all know of and have encountered many different types of leaders. There are literally hundreds of different styles, qualities, traits, etc., all with their own charts, diagrams and skill sets. What it comes down to is simple: you lead by example. Being in charge by having the most bugles doesn't make you a leader; it makes you a manager.

I was fortunate to have worked for four of the finest Battalion Chiefs in the Department, all with distinctively different styles, but with one thing in common: they all put their people first. All were well respected by the men and women who worked for them. Drennon Barton who I mentioned earlier was a big, iron-willed man with an energetic, follow me mentality and contagious laugh. Another was Mike Simons, who I never heard raise his voice, and rarely if ever had to mete out discipline. When Mike asked me to stay at Station 2 for one more year until he retired, I didn't hesitate to say yes. This prevented me from studying more for the Chief's test, but my respect for the man surpassed the necessity to get promoted. Dave Brooks; similar to Mike Simons in many respects and a man whose word was his bond. When I was first promoted to Lieutenant, I was given the choice to move to a slow station on "A" shift for six months or to change to "B" shift and stay at Station 2. When I said I would change shifts but I had family coming into town for Christmas and could not get the day off, Dave told me not to worry. True to his word, Dave worked with Mike Simons and had me moved back to "A" shift a few days before Christmas. Finally, Indelacio "Indy" Morgado, one of the most outstanding people I ever had the privilege and honor to know and work under. All four took care of their crews as if they were family, which they were.

"LIKE WINNING THE LOTTERY"

While working at Station 30 in Miami Shores one shift, a call came in for a multi-vehicle accident on U.S. Route 1, the cross-country highway that runs from Key West all the way to Maine. When we arrived, we found a new Porsche 911 that ran a stop sign and another car struck it broadside. The driver of the second car was uninjured since his airbag deployed. My Lieutenant, Chuck Lanza, who was also an RN, went to the passenger side of the Porsche while I approached from the driver's side. The patient was unconscious and police said that witnesses told them that he never braked or slowed down before running the stop sign. This led us to believe that the patient may have passed out before the accident. As we checked him for a pulse, we both realized that he had a weak carotid (neck), but no femoral (groin) pulse. This was a sign that he was bleeding internally and needed immediate surgical intervention. We secured his spine, loaded him into the rescue, and rushed him to the nearest trauma center. We started two large-bore intravenous catheters in route to be able to give him blood immediately. When we arrived, they rushed him into surgery.

He was lucky to have survived at all.

A few days later while at the hospital, we happened to see a member of the surgical team and asked how the patient did. The surgeon told us he had a ruptured abdominal aortic aneurysm (AAA) and received 37 pints of blood. According to research, the average mortality rate of an AAA during that time frame was 51 percent (Noel et al., 2001).

We also found out that the patient was also an orthopedic surgeon with privileges at that same hospital, and that he would make a full recovery. We never heard from him: it would have been nice but it wasn't expected.

"MOONS OVER MIAMI"

For several years, a few of the crews from Stations 2 and 7 would meet at the local community college stadium after our shifts were over, or if off-duty to exercise together and run the stadium steps. This was generally after running 25-30 calls during the shift, and if not being up all night, surely a good portion of it. What was also significant was that most of us were in our mid-to-late thirties and forties. We knew that fire doesn't care if you're twenty or fifty years old; it will treat you the same; not being in shape can get you or your partners killed.

While we were working out, the local Fire Academy would periodically have classes of recruits running from the academy to the stadium and back again. The instructors, who we all knew, would scream at the recruits to watch us and become inspired by our determination and work ethic. After hearing this repeatedly through multiple classes, we spontaneously decided to show our thanks for his continued support and proceeded to drop our shorts and moon the entire class of almost 40 recruits and the instructor.

The instructor who we actually had great respect for, shook his head and kept running. As good students should, they just kept running next to their instructor although several of the female recruits looked back once or twice.

"WAKE UP, WAKE UP!"

We all know what it's like to be behind the wheel and feeling drowsy. Sometimes, it's long hours at work; other times, it's being out too late, and unfortunately at times after imbibing too many alcoholic beverages. A bad idea on several levels. Notwithstanding, falling asleep while doing 40 mph or more in a two-ton battering ram is a recipe for disaster. In this particular case, the driver of a Lincoln Continental did just that: 45 mph right into the back of a church school bus that had stopped at a light. Fortunately, the bus sustained minimal damage and the kids who were onboard and headed to summer camp were unhurt. The Lincoln took a direct hit to the passenger side, taking out the windshield all the way to the back seat. The driver was shaken but relatively unscathed. I hope that the accident was a life-changing experience that both literally and figuratively woke him up.

Could have been much worse.

"90-MILE AN HOUR ONION"

For the most part, firefighters are professionals, role models, and mentors, but we can be a lot like kids. Again, many have Type "A" personalities and were adrenaline junkies long before they joined the fire service. It can be a necessity of the job as it many times consists of going from zero to 60 in just a few seconds, both physically and mentally. As has been stated throughout many of these stories however, we like to work hard and play hard. What has also been said, is that our lives depend upon one another. 85 to 90 percent of this job is getting along with one another. Camaraderie, both during the shift and afterward is not only common, but also necessary.

To that end, everyone takes a turn in the kitchen. Whether you can cook, barbecue, or pull something out of a pack and boil it, you are more often than not asked to cook a minimum of one shift every three weeks. The rest of the crews are responsible for cleanup on those nights. Although it may be one individual's turn to cook, the rest chip in with slicing and dicing the vegetables and generally preparing the meal.

This leads to what this chapter is all about; sometimes things get out of hand. In this particular case, there were a bag of onions in the station, and a few were being prepared as part of the meal.

Quite a few of our personnel had been college or pro athletes prior to joining the fire service. One or two made to the Major Leagues or to the NFL, and some had made it as far as Double or Triple A baseball. Once a conversation started to revolve around how good the arms were some on these guys, and if I recall correctly, some remarks were made (in fun) about our Lieutenant who happen to be a woman. This Lieutenant was Cindy Sears, who eventually became and deservedly so, the first female Assistant Chief in our department. Cindy was no slouch, and at one time had been a nationally recognized water polo player. She was also always up for a challenge.

Two of the guys in the crew, one being Manny Morales, started tossing around the onions like baseballs. One of them got tossed to Cindy, and someone made a comment about her not having a good arm. That's all it took; she reared back and fired that onion at the guys; they threw themselves on the floor and the onion hit the cabinets inches above their heads and exploded. There were pieces of onion all over them and the rest of the kitchen. With a smirk on her face, Cindy asked if anybody else wanted to test her arm, no takers.

"SMELLS LIKE FISH"

Like every other major urban department, and many other stations at Miami-Dade Fire Rescue, we had regulars, or what we call, "frequent flyers." These people call Fire Rescue several times a month or worse, several times a day. We had our fair share; actually, more than our fair share. So many in fact, we used to give the areas they lived in pet names; not so much the individuals, but the houses and streets that they lived on.

One of the originals was "The House of Idiots". It consisted of one large extended family. Some of them would eventually move, but not far enough away and unfortunately still in our territory. We now had the House of Idiots II, and even worse when a few others moved again, the House of Idiots III. We also responded to Mutant Avenue but that's another story in itself. Now when we say the House of Idiots, we're actually being too kind and insulting the characterization of idiot. With satirical tongue in cheek, I can confidently say with 99 percent accuracy that the cumulative IQ of the five or six people living in that house barely reached 100. We're not referring to people who are mentally challenged or have disabilities: we're simply talking about people who don't have a clue about what's going on (see the 80-20 rule).

In this particular story, we were called to the house once again for some inane complaint: one of many that Fire Rescues across the country are called for, day in day out. When we arrived (once again my Lieutenant was Cindy Sears), one of the women in the house met us at the door and said, "I smell like fish." As we were a little thrown off by that initial comment, we asked her to repeat it and explain what she meant. She proceeded to tell us that her vagina (although she did not use that particular word) smelled like fish. Now having seen these people on a regular basis, we knew that bathing was not part of their daily activities, and feminine hygiene was definitely something from a foreign language.

For some unknown reason, the television show Dragnet (Phillips, 2012), from the 1950s, and the lead character Detective Joe Friday played by Jack Webb came to mind. I asked, in my best Joe Friday voice and with a straight face, "What type of fish ma'am?" The woman looked at me dumbfounded, and Cindy started to roll her eyes. I repeated my question; "what type of fish ma'am? It's important to know as different disease processes smell like different fish. Is it kingfish or mackerel?" The woman looked at me with a vacant stare for what seemed like a few minutes and finally said, "I smell like mackerel." Cindy started to break out laughing but was able to keep it together. Suddenly, one of the other women walks into the room and yells, "I smell like fish too!" That's all it took; Cindy was gone.

"JUST HANGING AROUND"

One of the officers I learned the most from was Duke Adkinson. He was my Lieutenant on Rescue 2 when I first got to Battalion 5 and the one I mentioned in the head-on crash involving the tourists. A guy who grew up in one of the poorer sections of Miami and appreciated everything he had. He had brains and common sense, which unfortunately should be called rare sense. Eventually Duke became the Bureau Chief for Emergency Medical Services and was responsible for twelve EMS Captains and at the time, training at the time, over 700 paramedics.

One night I was at Rescue 7 with one of the other Captains, another old-timer who worked hard and played harder. We took one of the Captain's old jump suits and filled it with rubber gloves blown up with air. We used an old mop head as the hair and about 20 feet of webbing that one of the cops had given to us to tie it to one of the tow hooks underneath Rescue 2. We drove to Station 2 and the Captain and the other medic walked into the station. This was about 01:30 hours, so some of the crewmembers at Station 2 were getting ready to try to get some sleep before the next call. Duke and a couple of the other guys asked where I was. The Captain told them I had been disciplined for some minor infraction and was pissed off and wanted to stay outside. In fact, I was under their truck attaching the 20 feet of webbing to one of the hooks with the other end tied to the dummy. As luck would have it, a call for a sick person came in within five minutes of our being there. Since one of their crew was getting out of the shower, it gave us about a 10-second head start to get in our truck and wait for them to leave the station. They roared out of the Rescue bay with the webbing trailing behind. Suddenly, the dummy took off like a rocket, barely making contact with the ground. We followed behind, laughing so hard we could barely see. As they made the turn to head north to the call, the drunks that hung out on that corner were screaming that one of our guys was hanging on to a rope. When they arrived at the call almost two miles away, the dummy was still on the webbing and almost fully intact. The call turned out to be a false alarm. We tied the dummy to the front bumper of Engine 7 in a sitting position where it remained until someone stole it three weeks later.

"LOOKS LIKE A SUICIDE TO ME"

One of the County police officers requested Fire Rescue to respond to a scene to confirm a death, something that was done on a regular basis. Most of the officers were bright and street-smart, but just like our profession, there's always a few that don't have a clue. In this particular case, a car was "suspiciously" left near the projects. It was suspicious because cars left there didn't last long. Once the wheels and tires were stripped, the rest of the carcass was not far behind, losing the engine block, the seats, steering wheel, and whatever else could be cannibalized or pawned. When two adolescents popped the trunk to see what they could appropriate, they got the surprise of their young lives.

A suicide? Really?

Inside was a man hogtied with his hands and feet tied behind his back, a gag in his mouth, and several bullet holes in his body. As we were called to confirm that he was dead (several days dead with that distinct odor emanating from the trunk that could be smelled several feet away), I felt the need for just a tad bit of sarcasm. I told the cop who called us, "Looks like an obvious suicide to me." The officer, who was unquestionably new to the area and would rather be anywhere else, looked at me like a deer in the headlights. His colleagues just smiled.

"HELLO? CHUM?"

One shift we were preparing for a tropical storm that was expected to make landfall in South Florida, most likely somewhere in Miami-Dade County. We made a huge pot of spaghetti and another of ice tea and invited the cops in the neighborhood to stop by when they were on break. We were out on a call earlier that day and stopped in a gas station/bait shop to buy a couple of cokes. While we were in there, we noticed they sold five-pound blocks of frozen chum. For the uninitiated, chum consists of chopped baitfish and fish oils that are normally dumped overboard to attract, of course, fish. In this case, it was a five-pound block of frozen fish and fish guts.

Les Forster was my partner that shift, and while the boys in brown were in the station, Les and I pried off one front and one rear hubcap, placed about a one-half inch slice of chum in each and snapped them back on. Once they drove off, the heat from the brakes would promptly melt the chum, but the smell would definitely not go away. At first, the police thought that the prisoners who cleaned their cars were responsible; then they thought it employees of the local car dealership that repaired the vehicles.

When they found out we were the culprits, they wanted payback but the Police Major in the district at the time told them we were golden and therefore, untouchable. We had saved too many officers and been there for them again and again, and furthermore, he said it was one of the better practical jokes he had seen. We knew it was just a matter of time before they got back at us, or at least tried.

"BUT IT KEEPS HER WARM"

As we worked in a predominantly low-income area, some of the more frequent types of calls we received were for childbirths. During my almost 20 years working at Stations 2 and 7, I estimated that I had delivered or assisted in over 150 births. This doesn't include the close to 200 I was involved in working as a nurse or during my obstetrics rotation in nursing school (not my favorite call).

Many of the prospective mothers had no pre-natal care, health insurance, or transportation to the hospital, so many times the first and only exam they'd receive during the pregnancy would be by paramedics. On one particular occasion, the mother asked if we would take pictures for her during the delivery (in the back of the Rescue) and get them to her after she delivered. We told her it was no problem, took a series of photos as they baby was being delivered, made copies for ourselves and gave them to the mom. This was well before the Health Insurance Portability and Accountability Act (HIPAA) that provides safeguards to protect privacy existed.

Since we were two of the busiest stations in the country, EMT students or observers rode with us on a daily basis. At some time later, one of those observers, a police officer from one of the local municipalities, was assigned to our unit. He said he was trained as an EMT and needed ride time to keep his skills up. He and his agency will go unnamed for fear of embarrassment if he reads this as he obviously had not kept those skills current.

We told him that a new procedure of keeping a newborn warm was being beta-tested in the Miami area. With appropriate training, we would gently put the newborn back in the mother's vagina up to the neck until we reached the hospital. This was greeted with some skepticism and snickering but we insisted that this was factual and could prove it (we couldn't but it sounded good). We then showed him the photos but had conveniently reversed the order in which they were taken. His jaw slowly dropped open and said "Wow! That's amazing!" We never did tell him the truth.

"THE POPE COMES TO MIAMI"

In 1987, Pope John Paul II visited Miami to start his nationwide tour. President Ronald Reagan met with the Pope at Miami International Airport; afterward the Pope and his motorcade were escorted to downtown Miami for a parade, traveling through the city to a large park on the western boundaries of the County.

Two hundred fifty thousand members of the public and almost 5,000 political and religious dignitaries also attended. This was well before domestic terrorism was on the daily radar, but the threats of political assassination were still on the minds of local, state and federal law enforcement agencies since the attempt on President Reagan's life in 1981. Ironically enough, the Pope's outdoor Mass was scheduled for September 11, 1987, 14 years to the day prior to the attacks on 9/11.

Fire Rescue was a huge component of the response, but at that time, we were not considered part of public safety in the strictest sense and were present only to respond to medical issues. In anticipation of the crowds and the expected heat (84 degrees at 08:00 that morning), 11 first-aid tents surrounding the parking lot where the mass was held were set up, and more than 100 personnel from Miami-Dade Fire Rescue were assigned to work the event. I was assigned to take care of the throng of worshippers as a member of one of the dozen or so rescue squads in golf carts. Heat-related problems, minor cuts and bruises, a few broken bones, and one respiratory arrest added up to close to 100 calls for service in just a matter of hours.

The Pope traveled around the site perimeter in his Popemobile, a modified Mercedes-Benz ML430 with bulletproof Plexiglas, a built-in oxygen supply, and armor-plated side panels and undercarriage. It was accessed through the rear door and his chair was raised into place by a hydraulic lift. During the parade, he traveled in the vehicle with the Archbishop of Miami. As luck would have it, we were only 10-15 feet away from him when they passed our location. I was standing next to a Miami-Dade Police officer who I did not know, and in an apparent failed attempt at humor on an exceptionally hot day, I asked "so, which one's the Pope?" He glared at me and I realized that my humor went unappreciated.

"VICIOUS, AREN'T THEY?"

The area where we worked had a lot of stray dogs and cats. Because of their appearance and condition, they were known as "zone deer", and their average life spans ran about a year or so. When cats died, they were somehow able to find the proverbial burial ground, because we never saw their bodies. The dogs however, were a different story. Some had street smarts and were able to avoid getting hit by cars or trucks, but a good percentage of them didn't know a car from a tree and paid the ultimate price.

Picking up a dead dog from a busy street is not a priority item in most large urban areas and Miami-Dade County was no different. Unless it offended the senses of someone who was politically connected or the animal expired in a more affluent neighborhood, it lay there until animal control had time to pick it up. Some of the larger dogs, such as Rottweilers or shepherds died in positions that appeared terrifying at first glance: legs stiff, teeth bared, and eyes wide open. Once rigor mortis or rigidity due to biochemical changes sets in, the entire body stiffens.

The thing about working in busy houses is that when you have some free moments which are rare, you look for things to do to occupy your time. Therefore, on several occasions after running calls in the middle of the night, we would stop by one of these large dogs and stand them up in the medians. There was very little vehicular traffic, or those who were out in the middle of the night didn't know or didn't care what we did. For days, the dogs would draw stares from people using the main thoroughfares to get to work, and it gave us a few laughs at no one's expense.

"NO QUARTER"

Most of the people who stayed in Battalion 5 however, were quick-witted. We liked to play board games that required you to think, such as Risk or Trivial Pursuit. Every month, a game would be set up after station duties were completed and would typically take all day to finish as we continually ran calls between turns. Most of the time, the rescue crew played against the engine crew. At times, games would continue throughout the night, occasionally not being completed until the following shift. Sarcasm was also a large part of working there, and if you had a thin skin, you wound up leaving. None of this was ever malicious in nature, and now and then, we would turn on one of our own if the slightest mistake was made, either verbally or psychologically. Since no one's perfect, every one of us had his or her turn in the barrel, so to speak. It kept us sharp, built on the camaraderie, and best of all, forced everyone to learn something new.

"DIFFERENT UNIFORMS, SAME TEAM"

One early Friday evening, a call came in for a possible shooting several blocks from Station 7. Typically, a weekend night kept both police and Fire Rescue busy, and this night was no different. When we arrived, there was a victim in the street and an undercover Miami-Dade Police Department officer getting out of an unmarked car on-scene. The shooter appeared to be gone, and a friend of the victim was talking to the officer while we attended to the injured party who had a gunshot wound to the abdomen. We had him on the stretcher getting ready to load him into Rescue 7 when we heard a commotion behind us. Another individual arrived on the scene and began to argue with the victim's friend. The argument quickly escalated into a wrestling match and the cop attempted to break it up. This probably wasn't the best idea since he was only about 5'8" and the other two were over six feet tall. It was hard to tell what exactly what was going on and who was who, but it looked like the officer was not making any headway with the two six-plus footers. Worse, he became the focal point of one of the men who appeared to have his hand on the cop's holster and looked like he was trying to pull the weapon out while the cop was doing his best to hold on to it. Les Forster was pulling the patient on the stretcher out of harm's way while the Rescue Captain and I ran to help the police officer. The Captain and the officer took one guy down and subdued him. At this point, we didn't know who the bad guy was and really didn't care. Since I was taller and heavier than the other guy, I put him in a choke hold, wrapped a leg around both of his and dropped him face down on the pavement a la the sleeper hold (we were big fans of professional wrestling at the station) which knocked him out cold. Within minutes, half a dozen police units showed up to secure the scene, and we transported our patient to the trauma center. A few shifts later, the detective who was originally involved in the altercation showed up at the station to thank us, and to let us know that had we not stepped in, the situation would have definitely taken a turn for the worse. We joked with him saying that firefighters always take care of cops, but in reality, we always took care of each other, regardless of the organization you worked for or the uniform you wore.

"HERE SPOT"

One of the Captains who rotated through Battalion 5 on a CR cycle was a great guy but just a little obsessive-compulsive when it came to cleaning the station or the apparatus. We were very thorough at making sure the trucks were cleaned each morning, but when we were done, he would literally go through the truck again with rubber gloves to wipe down whatever we already cleaned. It wasn't an issue to him. He never complained about the job we did or asked us to clean it again; it just wasn't up to his personal specifications.

The Rescue and Squrt offices at Station 2 were combined into a 15' x 15' room at the entrance to the station and were the primary pass-through for anyone entering or leaving the station. This area was shared by both officers, printers, copiers, files cabinets, and chairs for civilians to sit on when having their blood pressures checked, usually a dozen or more times each day. This particular captain would always line up all the reference books and manuals on the shelves to make them look nice and neat. He would also straighten pencils, reports and anything else that looked out of place. Of course, I saw it as my responsibility to ensure that these items were then put back in disarray, therefore subscribing to the chaos theory (Thietart & Forgues, 1995).

We heard that this Captain had just purchased a Dalmatian pup that he would bring to Station 30 for fear of someone stealing the dog. Well, of course we saw this as a challenge as this clearly was meant to test us. For almost three weeks between calls, Lieutenant Bobby Schneider, Joe Starling and I cut pictures of dogs and various words and phrases out of magazines we brought in for a specific purpose. We spelled out a one-page ransom note, asking for a million dollars for the safe return of his dog's spots. We bought non-toxic white shoe polish and bided our time. When we finally heard Rescue 30 respond on a call, we jumped in Rescue 7 and headed over to their station. When we got there, the Engine 30 crew was in quarters and their Lieutenant said absolutely nothing but looked at us like, what are you crazy bastards up to now?

The ransom note.

The pup was in a training crate in the corner of the day room and extremely pleased to see us. We took him out of the crate, played with him and quickly started to white out his black spots. It wasn't as easy as we thought; it took more than one coat to block out the spots and was taking much longer than we expected.

When we heard Rescue 30 clear the call, we decided it was time for us to go. At that point, we only had about 90 percent of the spots washed out but were quickly running out of time to make our escape. We taped the ransom note to the front of the crate, put the pup back in, and said goodbye to him and the Engine 30 crew.

We expected to hear from the Captain that shift, but absolutely nothing. For several shifts, we anticipated an "I want you all in my office now" from our Battalion Chief but it never came. In fact, he never acknowledged what we did to anyone. We were somewhat disappointed not knowing if we drove him crazy that night.

"BREAD MAN"

The term sound likes a bakery company making a delivery, but in reality, Bread Man evolved from firefighters who are normally busy having no idea what to do when they have a few free hours. On the rare occasion that it was quiet in the station, someone would invariably sit down with a newspaper or magazine held high enough to present itself as a potential target.

One of the first objects used as a projectile launched through the reading material was a loaf of bread, hence the term, Bread Man. In time, several other items were used including vegetables, a mattress and one of our own, Manny Morales. This led to the variation known as Manny Man. The idea was to sneak up on the unsuspecting victim and yell "Bread Man!" at the point of impact. Bread Man Rules were as follows:

- Any individual of any rank could be targeted
  (be realistic, not stupid)
- Any reading material could be targeted
- The target must not have been in direct contact with the victim's lap or knees
- Any object, organic or inorganic could be used in place of bread (i.e., mattresses, onions, human beings); however, the use of small furry animals was discouraged

- Upon release of the object, the phrase "Bread Man" (or mattress man or other) must have been expressed in a clear voice, approximately 10-20 decibels above normal speaking tones or the current decibel level of the room (Station 2 "A" shift normally was at 90-110 decibel levels)
- A drumroll prior to release of the thrown object was considered a courtesy, and was not mandatory
- There was no limit to the number of times an individual could be subjected to Bread Man, either per shift or career

We would also let them know that Bread Man Rules were subject to change any time we felt like it.

One probationary firefighter who survived and was eventually promoted to Lieutenant set the record for being Bread-Manned three times within 45 seconds. After that barrage, he stood up for the rest of the shift, and I do believe he was afraid to go to sleep that night.

"MARKET WARS"

Most of the local Mom and Pop-type grocery stores in the primarily Black area where we worked were owned and operated by Arab-Americans. They generally had no ties to the local community other than their businesses, and the revenue was usually not re-circulated within the neighborhood. This didn't sit well with the community since prices were kept artificially high, and very few if any jobs were provided to the residents. For several years on the occasions when a new market tried to open, either locally owned or operated, or by competing Arab-Americans, they would be subject to spontaneously bursting into flames in the middle of the night. At least half-a-dozen grocery stores were firebombed or set on fire for insurance purposes.

On one occasion, the firebombing occurred while two employees were still inside. As they ran out, the assailants began shooting at them with handguns, forcing them back into the burning building. Their car, which was parked in front of the store, was also firebombed. Luckily, they were able to escape out the rear exit.

We received another call for a building fire early one morning, but when we arrived, the fire had blown itself out. When we made entry, we stepped in what appeared to be water on the floor, slipped and crashed to the floor. In his zeal to make sure the building would be leveled, the arsonist had poured gasoline into every container he could find; blenders, a popcorn machine, pitchers, and every other large container, not to mention the two five-gallon gas cans left on the scene, and the gasoline that was spilled on the floor. We quickly backed out of the store and had one of the crews use the booster line to wash the gasoline off our bunker gear. Had it reignited while we were still inside, there would have been several dead firefighters. This was before we knew better and gear had to be professionally cleaned. We cleaned the gear during our days off to get the gasoline out, but I'm sure that some of the contaminants were absorbed into the material's fibers and we continued to be exposed for years to come.

"THE 80-20 RULE (PARETO'S PRINCIPLE)"

The 80-20 Rule, also known as the Pareto Principle (Reh, 2016) or the law of the vital few, is commonly used in economics and the business world. It states that when an action that produces a certain response in the form of another action, approximately 80 percent of response come from 20 percent of the initial actions. In our world, it translates into 20 percent of the population providing for the other 80 percent in healthcare, transportation needs, and decision-making. The following describes one of those 80 percenters.

Note the tow truck driver in the background without protective gear!

In the late 1980's, an individual with a long rap sheet of minor convictions and run-ins with local police departments was visiting a convenience store to purchase some of his favorite liquid refreshments. While there, he got into a verbal confrontation with the driver of a tanker carrying liquid chlorine that had inadvertently blocked his vehicle. As the discussion got heated, the truck driver decided against the better part of valor and tried to leave with his cargo. The local individual who by this time had imbibed more than a few alcoholic beverages, decided to jump on the running board of the tanker, all the while attempting to break the window and get to the driver. After driving several miles into one of the neighboring municipalities, the panicked driver began to swerve and lost control of his truck. This resulted in the tanker overturning and throwing his would-be assailant to the ground. As it turned out, the attacker fell to the ground at the precise point where the tanker split, spewing its contents onto the ground and onto him. Since he was also partially pinned by the tanker, he was unable to escape the flowing chlorine that initially resulted in frostbite and subsequently emulsified his tissue. By the time responders arrived minutes later, he was dead: most likely from vapors he inhaled on contact or by being blended like a bar of soap. Not an easy way to go.

"THE SOUNDS
OF GUNFIRE"

In the 1980s and early 90s, the crews working along the 27th Avenue corridor which stretched from Station 2 on the south end to Station 11 in the north, were a little more aware of the possibilities of stray gunfire on July 4th and New Year's Eve, or worse, being directly targeted. Bullets coming from above were a common occurrence as individuals in the area or the neighboring municipality preferred to discharge their weapons as opposed to lighting fireworks. Every year or so, there would be reports of civilians struck by projectiles falling from the sky, causing injuries and the occasional fatality. One New Year's Eve, one bullet penetrated the roof of the cab of Rescue 2, striking the Captain in the shoulder. Fortunately, the deceleration caused by the metal roof slowed the fragment, causing minimal injuries.

One New Year's Eve, I brought a cassette player to work (popular in the 1980s, before the compact disc, but after the eight-track), put brand new batteries in it and put it in the bushes outside Station 7. Around 10:45 hours, I hit the record button and let it run. As our station fronted on 22nd Avenue and the dorms were in the front of the building, we tried to stay in the center or the areas away from the exterior of the structure to deflect or slow any potential direct hits. When we retrieved the machine the next morning, we played the tape and found almost three hours of close to never-ending gunfire. Single-shot, semi-automatic, shotgun blasts, and automatic weapons fire could be heard in rapid fire or spaced out, but never with more than one minute of silence. There were also hundreds of shell casings on the property in front of the bay doors, in the grassy areas, and around the perimeter. We were able to identify many of the weapons that were fired based on the different casings. About a week later, one of the guys went on the roof of the building for some work-related reason and returned with a dozen or so bullets or what appeared to be small metal fragments from weapons fire.

"CREMO"

Although everyone works in the same station, the same trucks, running on the same type of calls and customers day after day, each shift thinks there is a distinct difference between the personnel working 'A', 'B', and 'C' platoons. Nothing could be further from the truth: well, maybe just a little bit different. It is inevitable that individuals with idiosyncrasies as well as particular work ethics gravitate toward one another.

Our shift was no different. I've described many of the Type A+ characters that we had both at Station 2 and 7, and it's important to remember that this was long before energy drinks were even on the market. It's been documented that individuals with Type "A" personalities are bothered by anything that slows them down or wastes time (Macleod, 2014). They are overachievers, workaholics, are competitive, and have a low tolerance for incompetence. When you are a Type "A" and have down time, you do your best to fill that time productively. We would drill daily, especially with new personnel not familiar with the territory or the crews, review procedures, policies, and generally work on anything that would make us better at what we were paid to do; protect the public. Even with all of the above, the gallons of coffee and predator-prey mentality always had us thinking of ways to do more.

During one of our trips to the only large chain-grocery store in the neighborhood, an establishment we will not name due to its lack of cleanliness or safety measures, we came upon an oddity we had not seen before; ice cream with the tantalizing name of "Cremo." We were unfamiliar with this unique product and bought a one-half gallon; not for our consumption, but for the epicurean delight of our counterparts on the other shifts. Now our first clue to the quality of this item was that the average price of a one-half gallon of ice cream in the early 80s was about 89 cents while this excruciatingly exotic brand sold for 29 cents for the same size container. This ice cream was made in, packaged, and shipped from Thailand of all places. I didn't realize this until I recently researched the product in question. Now, I'm sure that the company produces fine goods and that this ice cream was considered imported when the company first went into business. During this time, however, the Food and Drug Administration apparently had a short period of collective amnesia and forgot their mission to protect and promote the public health. When we tasted a small spoonful of this facsimile ice cream, we almost gagged. The taste resembled a combination of cardboard with a hint of preservatives followed by the consistency of toothpaste. We had not intended to eat it but proposed to offer it as a sacrifice to our compatriots on the following shift. While at the store, we also bought a one-half gallon of Breyers that we consumed that night. Although many firefighters have the discerning taste of a pack of lions at a feeding frenzy, some have to be enticed into taking the bait and a bit of subterfuge is sometimes necessary. The Cremo was removed from its original container and placed into the now empty Breyers box. Two large scoops were unceremoniously dumped into the sink to give the appearance that someone had at least eaten one bowl of the Cremo in disguise.

In the majority of firehouses across the country, refrigerator day is a weekly occurrence. That day, all unmarked food, or food that doesn't specifically have someone's name and date on it becomes free game or is fated to be thrown out when the fridge is cleaned. Many firefighters become transfixed when there is the thought of a free meal and will eat almost anything that doesn't have a price attached to it. The "B" shift Rescue officer at the time was well-liked and very capable, but the word free was a huge part of his vocabulary, especially when it came to food.

As soon as he arrived at his normal time of 06:40 hours, he went right to the freezer knowing the shift was refrigerator day. When he spotted the box of unmarked Breyers, he laid claim to it and immediately scooped out a huge bowl thinking he hit the refrigerator day jackpot. He ate it as if it was his last meal on death row. When he finished it, he scooped out another huge bowl and marked it with his name, apparently saving it for later.

Several months later, this same officer was the focal point of another food-related prank. One of the firefighters working overtime brought a couple of dozen donuts to the station, and the powdered and jelly-filled, always the last to go, remained in the boxes like the last kid picked for a youth sports team. The doughnuts stayed in their boxes shift after shift and started to harden. No one wanted to eat them, but no one wanted to toss them either. We started to discuss whether the same officer, who had been off for a number of shifts, and was scheduled to return in two more days, would eat them upon his return. The consensus was that even he had his limits, and a side bet was made. I took that bet and formulated a plan. The day of his return was also a scheduled nuclear power plant exercise that included a mass decontamination at a local park. The officer in question was also a Hazardous Materials Technician scheduled to work the exercise.

Expecting a typical 90-degree South Florida day, we took the doughnuts with us to the park where they softened up in the heat. We left them on a table where they were clearly visible by multiple personnel. The sign in front of them said, "Free Doughnuts." Now going back to the expression that free is good, the other axiom is never trust a firefighter giving away free food. Most of us understand and adhere to that principle, but there's always one exception, and in this case, I knew which. He walked by, saw the sign and swallowed the hook. With a smile of pure satisfaction, he consumed at least three of the two-week old powdered donuts before moving on.

"LARGE RESPONSE TEAM"

Socioeconomic status has always had a strong influence on diet quality, and the underprivileged are typically forced to choose food options that lead to an overconsumption of calories and a rise in obesity rates (Darmon & Drewnowski, 2015). As a large percentage of the area we served was at or below poverty level, many of the residents were morbidly obese. We documented over 40 patients living in Station 2 and Station 7's territory that weighed more than 500 lbs. This was years before the advent of rescue vehicles and equipment designed to deal with bariatric rescues. Bariatrics is the branch of medicine that focuses on the causes, prevention, and treatment of obesity. These were not just people we happened to see during daily operations: these were patients we had run on at least once, and most of them, multiple times.

One weekend we responded to a call for difficulty breathing. When we arrived, we found a 26-year-old female who was having chronic breathing problems, primarily due to her excessive weight. She had been bedridden for approximately one year due to her tremendous size. This was not an acute life-threatening situation, but she definitely needed to go to a hospital for evaluation.

A truism in the world of pre-hospital care is that most patients will be found in the smallest room furthest from the front door.

A second proverb is that if it is a multiple-story building, either the elevator doesn't work, or they're in a building that by code is just able to avoid having an elevator installed based upon the height of that building, and by the way, the first rule still applies. This call fell into category number one; the smallest room furthest from the front door.

We found her on her bed with her stomach literally on the floor. She was lying on her side on a queen size bed and box springs without the frame, and her stomach was actually touching the floor! To make matters worse, she said her ankle hurt and she couldn't walk. It took us about ten seconds to assess the situation and realize that it would take more than just the three of us to move her onto the stretcher. We estimated her weight at well over 750 lbs.

I requested Squrt 2, Engine 7 and Rescue 2 for additional manpower. When they arrived, we figured that the best course of action would be to strap her to several backboards that we lashed together (she was too wide for the standard size backboard) and roll her out on top of multiple portable oxygen tanks. Since Captain Hal Sears (who I referred to earlier), and I were the two biggest guys, we strapped seatbelts over our shoulders bandolier style, and acted as the workhorses. Other firefighters would hook up to us and pull, while others would guide and push from behind. Since we had a limited amount of oxygen tanks, we would take the tanks from the rear and move them to the front, a la the Egyptians moving blocks to build the pyramids. The two smallest firefighters were assigned to rotate the oxygen tanks. While we were figuring out our strategy, the patient's father said she was trying to lose weight and was on a Slim-Fast diet. Hal said that was great, but she's not supposed to eat six months-worth at one time. It was tough, but we did everything to keep composed and professional.

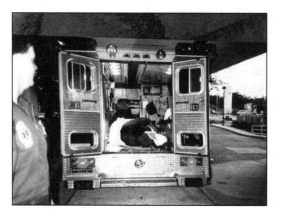

Wall to wall.

The first thing we had to do was get her out of the back bedroom. Two firefighters grabbed each arm to lift her and Gary Pilger, the Captain on Engine 7, climbed on the bed to push from behind to try to work her to the side of the bed. When he put his arms on her back, his hands literally sunk into her back up to his wrists. He yelled and pulled back, and we did all we could to keep from laughing aloud. We got back to work and eventually worked her over to the edge of the bed. We got her onto two backboards that had been doubled and strapped together to support her weight. When we attempted to pull her out of the room, we realized her fat was being hung up on the doorframes. At that point, we decide to strap additional back-boards to the opposing side, which made her look like a giant ice cream sandwich. Her flesh actually pushed between the handholds on the boards as we squeezed her through the doorway. After about 45 minutes of working her slowly to the door by rolling her over lined-up oxygen tanks, we realized the next step was somehow to get her into the Rescue truck. Four firefighters got inside to pull, while the rest of us angled the backboards onto the floorboard. We realized that we would have to remove the framework that locked the stretcher into place just to fit her in the truck. Eventually we were able to hoist the patient and the backboards onto the floor of the truck, but it was still a relatively snug fit as her immense girth came in contact with both interior walls.

The next step was getting her to the closest hospital and reversing the procedure. Getting her onto a hospital bed was easier said than done. In route to the hospital, we notified them of the type of patient and the fact that a standard emergency room stretcher would not be wide enough or strong enough to support her weight. When we arrived, they had a full-size hospital bed waiting for us at the emergency department entrance. We placed a canvas salvage cover on the floorboard prior to putting her in the truck, allowing all of us to drag her out of the truck onto the hospital bed. Positioning her on the bed was actually much easier than we anticipated. The problem was now getting her up the ramp, a standard one to 20-degree slope. As soon as we started pushing the bed with the patient on it (we estimated a total of about 1200 pounds), the wheel blew out, scattering bearings in every direction like bullets and triggering a brief moment of pandemonium. When it died down, we asked the hospital staff if they had a one or two-ton jack somewhere in the facility. The safety operations manager found one in a storage area, and we jacked up the damaged wheel high enough to wheel her into a patient care area.

We found out that she passed away from chronic respiratory complications three weeks later. They brought her to the Medical Examiner's office and as part of the autopsy, weighed her. Her weight after three weeks of being on a prescribed and limited diet in the hospital was 863 pounds.

"MO THE SHEEP"

An agricultural college that was built in our territory long before any of the residences, advertised "Live Chickens, $4.00". Every time we drove by, we saw it and thought about what we could do with a chicken. Since you couldn't beat the price, we decided to buy two of them and put them in the Engine 7 Captain's locker just before he opened it. The chickens wouldn't be harmed and would be returned to the college unscathed as soon as the prank was over.

We drove onto the college grounds and found the main office. When we explained to the supervisor what we wanted the chickens for, he suddenly became serious and asked "How about a steer?" "Too big", we told him. His next offer was a full-grown pig. Unfortunately, the pig was close to 400 lbs. and would be more trouble than it was worth. He then suggested a sheep. For some reason, we immediately thought of a cute little lamb no more than 20 to 30 lbs., so we said that would work.

He had us drive to the back of the acreage and one of the students came out with this sheep on a leash. This so-called lamb was a full-grown ewe that weighed in at about 150 lbs. Being firefighters, that last thing we wanted to do was to show these guys that we couldn't handle it, so we told them the sheep was perfect.

The kid holding the sheep said her name was Mo, and if he knew we were coming, he would have had her ready. We weren't quite sure what he meant and thought the worst, but it turned out he meant he would have washed her and fed her. As it was, they gave us a container of food and we promised to bring her back safe and sound before they closed the shop at the end of the day.

Now the fun part was trying to get Mo in the back of the rescue truck. My partner Joe Starling, was in the truck holding the leash and the Lieutenant and I had our shoulders in the sheep's hindquarters, pushing it into the truck. Firehouse 7 was only about a mile from the agricultural college and we figured we could get back there in a few minutes at worst. Of course, this wasn't meant to be. Not 30 seconds after clearing the college grounds, we were dispatched on a seizure in Station 2's territory, roughly four miles away. We were trying to figure out how we were going to explain having a sheep in the back of the truck when we arrived, but Engine 7 was just clearing from a run in the south end of our territory and took the call, saying they would advise if they needed Rescue to roll in. We flew back to the station as fast as possible and brought Mo inside.

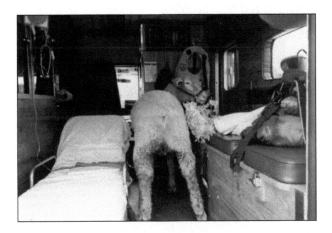

Mo in the back of Rescue 7.

Now, Station 7 was one of the smallest firehouses in the County. It was no bigger than your average two-bedroom house, including the engine bay that opened onto a side street, and the rescue bay which opened directly onto a six-lane main road. We let Mo walk around the day room, which consisted of seven chairs that you used to find in a dentist's waiting room, a side table and a television. If you fell backward out of your chair, you'd literally wind up in the kitchen/dining room that could possibly hold up to four people at a time unless we were sitting down at a picnic bench that served as our dining table.

Our main concern was that we would be on a call and our Battalion Chief (we had reorganized by this time and the Battalion Captains were promoted to Battalion Chiefs) would be making rounds and open the front door by the main road with traffic speeding by. If Mo got out this door, she'd become lamb chops and we'd be dead meat. The next best thing was to put Mo in the engine dorm. Mo immediately went to one of the firefighter's cubicles and started to eat his county-issued red bedspread.

Just visiting!

At this point, I don't know why, but I started thinking about the bowel habits of sheep. I vaguely remembered that sheep manure was more or less like small pellets and volunteered to clean up if Mo saw a necessity to eliminate waste. I quickly made eye contact with Joe who caught on and agreed to do the same. The Lieutenant, obviously thinking it would be straightforward and much less difficult, said he would clean up if the sheep decided to urinate on the rug. It didn't take long before Mo dropped a few pellets here and there. I cleaned them up and she did it again. Joe and I took turns picking up the pellets when a few minutes later, Mo decided to let loose with a stream of urine that looked like someone had kicked over a 55-gallon drum of some foul-looking chemical. The Lieutenant was screaming and cursing at the sheep, at us, and everything else, but got down on his knees and started to clean up the urine. He could have easily ordered us to clean up but he manned up and fulfilled his part of the agreement.

About 20 minutes later, Engine 7 cleared their call and came back to the house. One of the firefighters who was assigned to us that day came in first and headed straight for the dorm. When she opened the door, she looked down and Mo looked up at her. There was dead silence and a staring contest ensued for about 15 seconds until she said, "Cap, there's a sheep in the dorm." The Captain, Gary Pilger had come from the airport years before (another story) and decided to stay with this nutcase group for almost 14 years. Nothing fazed him anymore, and his answer was a simple, "Why am I not surprised?" We offered to take some career-ending photos of Gary standing in his fire boots with Mo's back legs in the boots with him, but he politely declined.

Several years later when I was promoted to Division Chief, we were attending the grand opening of one of our new stations. As I was telling the story, the Fire Chief walked up and joined the conversation. One of my colleagues, another recently promoted Division Chief, was behind him and was frantically motioning for me to stop but I figured I had nothing to hide. As you've probably figured out, I'm not very politically correct and don't have much of a filter. If the Chief demoted me, so be it. From what I knew of him, I assumed nothing would happen. He was a man I greatly respected because he put the fire-fighters first. As I continued to tell the story, he listened intently and didn't say a word until I was done. Then he looked me in the eye and said, "That's nothing. I had an elephant in my station." He then went on to say that when he was a firefighter in a local municipality, a small Mom and Pop circus came to town and set up shop next door to one of their firehouses. The circus had a couple of elephants, including a baby. He and his crew asked the owners if they would allow them to bring the baby elephant to their station and apparently, the owner had no problem with the request. They brought the elephant next door, through the day room and into the dorm. The elephant saw no reason to go around partitions and instead, knocked down everything in his path. According to the Fire Chief, the Captain who was in his dorm, never got off his bed and never raised his voice but said "Get that f***in' elephant out of my house."

Still in my Class "A" uniform (long-sleeve and tie), I dropped to my knees and bowed with my hands over my head and said, "You are like a god to me." When he started to laugh, I knew I was keeping my badge.

"A CHRISTMAS STORY"

Duke had a great sense of humor. Very dry, but he appreciated a good practical joke when the time was right. When I first got on the department, the dormitories in the houses were wide open, without any privacy. With more and more women being hired, management wisely decided to put cubicles inside the dorms, providing some semblance of privacy. They were nothing fancy, just drywall with paint on them. The layout in the dorm at Station 2, a room approximately 11' x 16' had two beds side by side, with another bunk centered across from them next to a storage room. This allowed for a "T" shaped wall between the first two cubicles.

Before Christmas one year, Duke and I bought manila file folders, covered the entire wall and drew a reproduction of a brick wall around a fireplace. To add to the ambiance, we found an old stuffed chair and small broken table in a trash pile which we placed in the corner of the dorm and put a radio on the table to play Christmas music. A glass of eggnog was added and we realized only one thing was missing; a dog by the fireplace. And so, we went out and brought back a dog of unknown heritage that had been dead for several weeks and flattened out. This made it easy to carry the dog back to the house, as it only weighed about one or two pounds. The perfect traditional Christmas scene.

"COOL AND CREAMY"

Another call Duke and I ran on was a report of a possible allergic reaction. When we arrived, we found several individuals of various ages sprawled around a room with one of their friends complaining that he drank a Pepsi and was having an allergic reaction. He obviously wasn't; his vital signs were normal and there were no signs of a rash or any swelling. He did appear to be itching due to rolling in the grass and had a good deal of alcohol on board. We figured this out as there were at least two dozen empty beer and liquor bottles spread across the room. We knew this as our law enforcement friends told us that this is known as a "clue."

Duke quickly told one of the friends to get shaving cream and spray it on his buddy's back. His friend decided if one can was good, two canisters must be better. Once he had about two inches of shaving cream covering his back, he said he never felt better. Just to keep them busy, Duke told his friend not to take his eyes off him for several hours. We had him lay face down in the back seat of one of their cars and sent him to the County Hospital.

"BAD GUYS DON'T DIE"

Several weeks later, an ex-convict just released from Dade County jail broke into a car owned by a police officer, stole a handgun, and carjacked another vehicle in the courthouse parking lot. A high-speed chase ensued through several residential neighborhoods, ending in a multi-car accident when the bad guy blew a red light. We arrived on the scene along with three other rescue units, and found several people including a couple of kids with minor injuries both in and out of their cars. The cops had surrounded the car with weapons drawn and the felon still behind the wheel. As we were closest to the perpetrator, the other crews provided care for the victims and we decided to handle the bad guy. Along with the police, we grabbed the guy through the broken window and yanked him out. We threw him onto a backboard, immobilized him, more for security purposes than patient care, and took him to the hospital under heavy police guard.

Not surprisingly, this nasty piece of work received only scratches after crashing a car at over 60 mph. As I said earlier, the general rule at the time and has remained so to this day is, "Bad guys don't die and drunks don't get hurt in accidents." Unfortunately, the opposite also occurs. Good people suffer the consequences and either die or become severely injured as in the purse-snatcher incident or get killed or maimed by drunk drivers. No matter how careful you may be, how smart you are, or the precautions you have taken, you can never completely avoid being in the vicinity of those who couldn't care less about the welfare and well-being of others.

"FREE BRAIN CELLS"

Jackson Memorial Hospital (JMH) was, and still is the County Hospital. Almost everyone without insurance eventually found his or her way there for medical care. Most hospitals nowadays are used as a clinic or everyone's private doctor for everything including colds, headaches, stomachaches and the like. Even then, Jackson's Emergency Department was the first choice for people who didn't bother to go to the appropriate clinic for appointments because they didn't want to wait the two or three days until they could get in to be seen. Many would call Fire Rescue with the mistaken idea that if we took them to the hospital, they would be seen by a physician that much faster. To this day, a number of people think that the 911 is there for their personal use.

One such citizen under the influence of several bottles of fine wine with screw off tops, called us to request a ride to get a place to sleep it off for the night. We had come into possession of a few dozen expired "preferred customer" cards from a local furniture store and advised this individual that he did not need Fire Rescue to transport him, only to present one of these cards to jump ahead of everyone else in line. We told him that free brain cells were being given out for a limited time upon presenting this card. Out of the alley came a voice, "I want some free brain cells too!" The drunken friend was given a similar card, and both off went to the hospital, presumably to increase their intellectual capacity. It's too bad we didn't get to see the end results when they presented the cards to the emergency department staff.

"FIRE ALARM BOX"

After clearing from a call late one night (or early the next morning) we were driving back to Station 2 when we noticed a Bellsouth truck parked on the street. Bellsouth was one of the seven original regional phone companies formed after AT&T was broken up. We pulled over to make sure the technician was okay and asked what he was doing working so late. He told us all the fire alarm boxes were being removed from service and he was taking them down. When we asked what he was going to do with them, he answered that the boxes would probably be trashed, but hinted that if they were gone by the time he got to that particular spot, then it would make his job that much easier.

Still operational.

We got the message and quickly went to the next box about 300 yards away. I climbed on top of the rescue and separated the phone from its harness, chopping the last set of wires with an axe. As soon as I got back on the ground, we got another call, then another, then another. When we returned to take down two more boxes, they were gone as was the Bellsouth technician. Duke and Gene were shut out but I have the box to this day. A collector's item and antique to boot, at least 60 years old and still functioning quite nicely.

"THE PRICE OF GAS... AT BOTH ENDS"

We responded to a call of difficulty breathing and upon arrival, found a woman sitting near a small oscillating fan with her mouth wide open trying to inhale as much as air as possible. When asked what the problem was, she replied that she had a lot of gas for the past week and was trying to replace it with fresh air. Joe Starling had already begun checking her blood pressure and was on one knee next to her with the stethoscope in his ears. As I was checking her pulse and respiratory rate, I asked her if she had tried belching. She said no, so I told her to see if that would help. She turned her head in Joe's direction and let loose with a belch that came from deep within her bowels. He virtually collapsed from the stench of her breath, which we could smell across the 8' x 10' room. As he stumbled to his feet and backed away, I asked the patient if she felt any difference and she said "Yes, much better." I told her to try passing gas and see if that would help. My Lieutenant, Cindy Sears who I'd mentioned in several earlier stories was on the other side of the bed, realized what was happening and started to work her way around toward the door, shuffling sideways between the bed and the furniture. Joe and I quickly exited the room and held the door shut behind us as the patient began to alternately belching and farting saying, "I feel so much better!" The Lieutenant meanwhile, was cursing at us while desperately trying to open the door and avoid the noxious fumes emanating from both ends of the patient.

"FAST NAP"

One of my partners at Station 7 was Steve Hondares, the same guy who saved Manny Morales life (more about that later). Steve was a hard-working, no-nonsense type of guy when it came to work but had a great sense of humor and was one of the most outstanding firefighters I ever met. This guy wouldn't take a sick day if his arm were cut off. One day during a rare breather in running calls, he decided to lie down for a nap. About an hour later, Steve comes out of the dorm limping. We asked him what had happened, thinking he fell off the bed or banged it against one of the lockers. Steve said he was dreaming about running, and apparently sprained it during his nap. After we finished laughing our asses off, we realized that he actually had a swollen ankle. Talk about the power of the mind!

"DON'T BRING A SPORTS CAR TO A TRUCK CRASH"

We in South Florida have the dubious distinction of having more motorists who drive without a license, drive with suspended or revoked licenses, and/or those who leave the scene of an accident, especially with injuries. In addition, our state governmental agencies had the exceptional foresight to stop requiring vehicles to pass an annual inspection, putting thousands of cars and trucks on the road with bald tires, bad brakes, and spewing emissions into the air or oil onto the roadway. Unfortunately, this was not limited to surface streets, but includes the expressways and major thoroughfares. One of those roads is U. S. 27, or as it was and still is more commonly referred to as, "Bloody 27", one of the most dangerous in South Florida. The speed limit is 55 mph (which translates to 70 plus mph in Miami), and crossing traffic has to guess if they can make it across the road safely, especially those junctures that only have stop signs. Motorists traveling through the western reaches of Miami-Dade County, many times failed to judge the speed of oncoming vehicles as they tried to pull into traffic or cross at one of the few available intersections.

She walked away from this one.

A countless number of accidents, many with fatalities occurred on this stretch of highway, with the majority being high impact from behind, T-bones, or head-on wrecks. We responded to a multi-vehicle accident involving two dump trucks and two passenger vehicles at one of the intersections that did have a light. A fully loaded tractor-trailer with bald tires and bad brakes (thank you, State of Florida) ran into two cars stopped at one of the red lights behind a dump truck. The first car that was hit was a Mazda Miata convertible driven by a young lady. Somehow, the Miata was squeezed out of the pileup and shot out like a watermelon seed, ending up in the median. Amazingly, the driver only suffered some minor abrasions and was able to walk away from the crash although the car sustained significant damage.

The driver of the second vehicle, a heavy older Cadillac was not as fortunate. The car was flipped up on end and pushed into the dump truck, folding it like an accordion in a trash compactor. The woman inside the Cadillac was killed instantly: she was pushed up against the firewall as the second truck crushed the entire passenger compartment on and around her. Ironically, the tractor-trailer that rear-ended her vehicle had a large smiley face painted on the sides which gave the entire scene a surreal appearance. The Cadillac's driver's body was so tightly compacted in the wreckage that she couldn't be extricated without doing additional damage. The car and its occupant had to be loaded onto a flatbed truck and transported as one to the Medical Examiner's office.

A truly bizarre scene.

"HE'S HALFWAY THERE"

In the early 1980's, a call came in one sunny Sunday afternoon for a possible 20-something female drowning in a lake near one of the local hospitals. As many of us were SCUBA-trained rescue divers, it just so happened that Rescue 7 and Rescue 30, the two nearest Rescue units both had two divers each on their crews. Rescue 7 arrived first and we could see the victim about 30 yards offshore treading water. When she saw us, she actually started swimming away toward a small manmade island in the middle of the lake. My Lieutenant and I went into the water with lifelines and rescue buoys. While we were in the lake, she made it to the island and climbed a tree.

Personnel from the hospital next door arrived and advised us that the individual had just been released from the psychiatric wing and was in the midst of surgical intervention to change him from a man to a woman. Now in the 80's, this was uncommon to say the least, and drew a considerable amount of attention when made public. Again, this was prior to the implementation of the HIPAA Act of 1996. My Lieutenant had very little empathy for emotional issues and was strictly a get-the-job done kind of guy. It made no difference to him that the patient was a transsexual: he just didn't put up with the BS of tying up resources by someone looking for sympathy.

As one of the four divers, I remained in the water several yards offshore while the Lieutenant climbed on shore and gestured several times for the individual to come down out of the tree, each time being ignored or refused outright. He finally had enough and told the patient to climb down from the tree or he would knock her out of there with a fist-sized rock that he had picked up. The message was instantly understood, and the patient came down from her perch. The Lieutenant secured her with a lifeline and a buoy and once back in the water, handed her over to me. I started to swim toward shore with the victim in tow and my officer right behind. Rescue 30 had now arrived and expected to assist in saving a young lady in distress. We shouted to them as they were dressing out on shore but conveniently neglected to provide certain details such as the topic of gender identity. It was unnecessary but yelled that we would hand off the patient at the approximate midpoint back to shore. One of the paramedics on Rescue 30 was a former professional football player who loved the ladies and they loved him. When I handed the patient over to him, he quickly put her into the cross-chest carry and began swimming back to shore. When he got back to shore with the victim, he was ready to give interviews to the media for the heroic job he performed. When I took off my dive gear, I leaned over and quietly inquired if he had asked the victim out on a date yet. He replied that he hadn't, but he probably would. I decided to burst his bubble and tell him that she had been a he. His jaw almost hit his chest and he bolted for his truck, getting out of there as fast as possible.

"PRANK MENTALITY"

As I said earlier, every house has its own individual identity and each shift even more so. No matter where you work, personnel who think alike, have the same work ethic and the same sense of humor, and have a habit of gravitating toward one another. There will always be exceptions, but for the most part, you're living with your second family, a group of people who are in the same firehouse for 24 hours, every third day. As I said, getting along is 90 percent of the job; otherwise you don't belong and should consider another career.

With that said, pranks are a mainstay of the fire service, particularly in the busier houses. This provides an outlet for all of the death, misery, trauma, and emotional baggage we encounter and take on personally every shift. Pranks are acceptable but only under a rigid set of parameters: no harm comes to anyone, physical or otherwise; no property is damaged; and finally, if you're willing to be part of the practical joke, you'd better be ready to be the victim of one and not take it personally. Most firefighters understand and adhere to these boundaries, but there are always a few that like to be the instigator but not the butt of the joke. Many of the following stories involve practical jokes on fellow firefighters.

"WELCOME TO STATION 7"

Early in my career at Station 7 we had an ongoing change of personnel through promotions, especially at the Captain level. As I said earlier, Gary Pilger, who had recently been promoted worked at Miami International Airport for many years. Once he was promoted to Captain, one of the stations he was assigned to was Station 7. After working there for several shifts, he realized that his job there consisted of getting to the truck and writing the rescue or fire report; his crews were that good at their jobs.

Gary got the bid for the Captain position at Station 7. However, he was not used to the multitude of Type "A" (MacLeod, 2014) personalities working in Battalion 5. When we had some downtime, or weren't running calls, we had a tendency to do things that weren't considered "normal" in other areas of the fire service, and certainly not in the private sector.

However, regardless of where you work, people have a tendency to develop routines. One of our routines consisted of drinking up to eight pots of coffee per day, starting around 06:15 hours, and continuing until midnight or later. We never expected to have down time or to be able to rest during the shift, so we were ready to be up for the full 24-hours. Gary's first shift at Station 7 was one to remember, at least for him. While he and his crew were out drilling, the rescue (with the full endorsement of his crew) removed the Captain's bunk. I mean, we literally took his mattress and box springs out of his assigned cubicle and hid them. The mattress went into the back of one of the crews' station wagons (SUVs didn't exist in the early 80's), and the box springs were hidden in a loft where extra equipment was stored. Around 02:00 hours, the Engine crew jumped into their bunks in order to try to get an hour or two of shuteye. Gary, being the good Captain, was completing the last of his many reports and was the very last to go into the engine crew dorm. The rest of his crew pretended to be asleep, and Gary went by them quietly in the dark to get to his cubicle. When he got to his cubicle, and flipped on the night light, he realized his bed was missing.

Now Gary bid Station 7 with his eyes open; there were no surprises as our reputation preceded us. He knew what to expect from the guys and that we were not only Type "A" personalities, but in some case, "AAA plus." To his credit, he didn't make a lot of noise, and he didn't try to wake anyone up. However, he started quietly huffing and puffing, and the guys in the engine dorm were jamming pillows over the mouths to keep from laughing. He left his cubicle, walked down the hall, and went outside to search for his bed. Once they heard the door close behind him, they busted out laughing. After searching for about 20 minutes, he gave up and decided to go to sleep in the recliner. Again, to his credit, the good Captain never mentioned the incident and went about his business. When we did tell him the truth several shifts later, he smiled and knew that he had been accepted into the Battalion brotherhood.

"NO GOOD DEED GOES UNPUNISHED"

I mentioned Steve Hondares a few times; one of the best firefighters I ever had the honor to work with. Steve was a gung-ho type of guy but definitely had a soft side. Early one Sunday morning we got a call for a trailer fire. Not a big deal, there was heavy smoke but minimal damage to the structure: no occupants or owners on-scene. However, we discovered that three Shi-Tzus were inside and had been overcome by smoke inhalation. I thought that all three dogs were dead but Steve found a pulse on the first, then the other two. He decided he wanted to work the dogs but there were no oxygen masks designed for pets back in the 80's. He fashioned a contraption that allowed them to get what we call "blow-by" oxygen; no mask for the face, but enough oxygen to make a difference. As it turned out, the dogs started to respond one by one. Unfortunately, they had been without oxygen for a considerable amount of time and started actively seizing. Once they started having seizures, they lost control of their bowels and began to leave doggie deposits on the stretcher. Steve first looked at me, then the officer, and we both shook our heads and told him, "Your decision, they're yours to deal with." We told the cops that when the owners returned to let them know we were driving to the nearest animal shelter. The shelter was only a couple of miles away, and although not open for business, was still staffed. When we got to the gate, we hit the air horn and siren several times before we were able to get the attendant's attention. Meanwhile, the dogs' seizures were continuing, and Steve was trying his best to keep them from crapping all over the rescue truck. The attendant finally came out and told us there was no way he could take the dogs, as he was the only one on-duty.

Steve has his hands full!

Our answer was simple; we couldn't ride around with three dogs in a Fire Rescue vehicle and regardless of being short-handed, he was best equipped to handle the situation and let us get back in service. It wasn't stated in such eloquent terms but he got the message. He relented; we handed over the three dogs and let Steve finish cleaning the truck before the next call.

"HERE KITTY, KITTY, AND KITTY"

Most stations have a kitty, or a fund that all personnel contribute to on payday to cover the cost of items over and above what each department provides. We actually had three separate kitties; one for the newspaper, condiments, cable TV, etc; a second for coffee, and a third for tools.

Working out of Stations 2 and 7 as well as many of the other busy stations across the County such as 3, 9, 11, 16, and 29 was a badge of honor. We had a friendly competition with other crews and stations, within both MDFR and our neighboring cities. Every one of us thought we were the busiest and best station with the most calls, and better firefighters and medics than the other guys were. I know that this is no different from most departments across the country, but I can only speak for the houses where I normally worked. These bragging rights sometimes drilled down to the shifts themselves.

The crews at many of the busier houses such as Station 2 went as far as to buy equipment or tools that either weren't available through the department or (cough, cough) even authorized to use. We had a separate tool kitty specifically for this purpose. When someone worked overtime as described earlier, the general rule was that each would pay $5.00 or bring ice cream. Some stations preferred ice cream, but we always requested the money.

One of the tools we bought was a pneumatic air chisel. We kept one of our 2200-psi air bottles secured to an extra Self Contained Breathing Apparatus (SCBA) harness as a ready air supply. We also moved some of the equipment around on the Rescue to give us more space to store additional SCBA bottles for the chisel. We built wooden shelves specifically for the bottles and used metallic gray fleck stone spray paint to make it look like it was a factory installation. Another piece of equipment we bought was a cordless 24-volt reciprocating saw and we were working on purchasing a chain saw when I left.

Now for the coffee kitty: as I wrote earlier, we drank coffee, a lot of coffee. I didn't drink my first cup of coffee until I was 32 years old and on the fire department. When I first tasted it, I thought, "Are you kidding? It tastes bitter and has an aftertaste. Who'd drink this garbage?" I soon found out; me. When I first worked in Battalion 5 and specifically Station 2, I couldn't believe that Duke and Gene drank a glass, not a cup of coffee on almost every call leaving the station. This was anywhere from 20-30 glasses a day. They also smoked cigarettes going to every call. Back then, not only were we not smoke-free for a year prior to being hired, but personnel were allowed to smoke in the apparatus when not on a call. It's a wonder I didn't start smoking as well. Soon afterward, I started drinking coffee, a little at first, a lot toward the end.

We averaged eight pots, not cups, but entire pots of American coffee every shift for eight people. Once in a while, other crews would come by for training or for a visit, and an extra fresh pot was brewed. Add to the mix that in South Florida, we also drink Cuban coffee.

Cuban coffee is known affectionately as Cuban crack, jet fuel or any of a hundred other terms of endearment. Cuban coffee is twice as strong as American coffee and ridiculously sweet and is either sipped or downed like a shot. The primary ways we drink it is as a Colada, which is a small plastic cup consisting of a single shot, or from a large Styrofoam cup, with a stack of small plastic cups, enough for all your friends. Three to four of these during a shift plus all the other coffee and it was no wonder we stayed up all night.

"FOOD FOR THOUGHT"

A few firefighters either forgot or would not put their gear away after their shifts. To miss once or twice was forgiven: any more than that opened the door for retribution. In general, these were individuals assigned for one or two shifts, or worse in their eyes, filling a position for up to six months. Either way, they didn't want to be there. In this case, this was one of our bid-in regulars; a guy we all liked, but who was slightly forgetful at times. This happened on several occasions, so we decided to teach him a lesson. He left his bunker boots in the corner of the day room so we filled them with grated cheese, mustard, and broken up garlic bread from a previous meal.

It just so happened he was off for a few shifts, so by the time he got back, the contents of the boots were incredibly ripe. Nevertheless, in true firefighter fashion, he took it well. Apparently, on his first shift back they had a fire right at shift change; he took a deep breath, put his feet into the concoction and went to work. He did say that most of the guys kept their self-contained breathing apparatus SCBA on around him well after the fire was extinguished but he never forgot to put his gear away again. For the next month or two he smelled like a garbage can that sat outside an Italian restaurant.

"SALAD DAYS"

As I said, many firefighters refused to take promotional exams out of anxiety of moving out of their comfort zones and possibly being assigned to Battalion 5. Others did not mind and saw it as preferable to bouncing around the County as unassigned or float personnel. Many of those individuals elected to ensure that their gear remained as clean throughout their careers as it was coming out of the box when it was first received, even before the NFPA ratified Standard 1851, Selection, Care, and Maintenance of Protective Ensembles for Structural Fire Fighting and Proximity Firefighting in 2001. One such paramedic thought that the personnel on the rescues should remain outside burning buildings and work only as Medical Sector, not as fire companies. This particular Lieutenant had a habit of leaving his fire helmet out of his gear locker in the Rescue bay.

Manny Morales and I took the leftover salad from dinner, filled his helmet and put it in the freezer. He said nothing; no complaint made, no threats, nothing! We were a little disappointed, and all this did was embolden us. The next time he did it we dug up a small tree in a lot near the station, planted it in his helmet and placed soil around it. It was actually quite impressive! Of course, he went ballistic and made a complaint, but our Battalion Chief wanted to know why his helmet which belonged to the County property was not stored properly. The Lieutenant dropped the complaint and eventually went elsewhere. Of course, this officer followed the "Peter Principle" and quickly promoted through the ranks.

"DO THE HOKEY POKEY"

We ran dozens of calls at the Northside District 2 police station, thankfully with the majority of calls for the prisoners, not the officers or staff. Most of the calls were in the holding cells for individuals who claimed to feel ill or have some underlying medical problem such as rectal-cranial inversion or cranial rectitis (both referring to heads up their asses), but the bottom line was that they didn't want to go downtown to the County jail for an overnight stay or longer.

One such inmate claimed some vague illness. We checked his vital signs, performed an electrocardiogram, and found absolutely nothing wrong. At that point, I told the prisoner we would check for neuromuscular anomalies. My crew knew something was up but acted as if this was a normal examination and went along with it. I asked him to sit upright and put his right foot underneath him. I then asked him to put his right foot out in front of him and shake it. Then I told him to put him to first put his left foot in, and then to put his left foot out. I had him shake it all about, turned to the officer and said, "And you turn yourself around, that's what it's all about." The officer who didn't know us had a perplexed look on his face but both of my guys and three of the veteran cops lost it. Even the prisoner thought it was funny.

"NEW TO THE NEIGHBORHOOD?"

As with Fire Rescue, you had a number of police officers who were attracted to the Northside District for the action: shootings, stabbings, multi-vehicle wrecks and trauma were the norm. Other officers would be assigned to the district and definitely felt uncomfortable with the clientele, and left for safer, quieter environments as soon as their seniority allowed.

One such officer had just completed his probationary period and was assigned to the night shift. Typically, all the rescues were running, as were the police units. A call came in for a man down and we responded with the sound of police sirens in the distance. When we arrived, we found a homeless man squatting down, leaning against a wall with his pants down around his knees. The gentleman was finishing a bowel movement on a newspaper when the newly minted police officer arrived at the scene.

We could tell he was new to the area for several reasons. First and foremost, the cops in the area would not run with sirens after midnight unless it was a dire emergency. You didn't want to wake up any other potential callers, and you didn't want to alert anyone you were in route if the perpetrator was still on-scene. Secondly, the officer was in a crisp, newly pressed uniform, and as it turned out, this happened to be his first or second day on the job riding solo. Thirdly, he had on a pair of dress shoes as opposed to the standard tactical work boots preferred by Fire Rescue and law enforcement. I happened to be squatting down in front of our homeless friend, a safe three feet away on a slight rise on the concrete sidewalk when the officer decided to let this miscreant know that he was breaking the law by defecating in public. Our down-and-out acquaintance looked the cop square in the eye, grabbed the pile of steaming solid waste with his bare hand and backhanded it against the storefront wall. The cop's eyes got big and his mouth dropped open, but he failed to realize that the derelict had also started urinating, which was running down the sidewalk straight at the officer's new shoes. When the cop realized that he was now standing in a puddle of urine, we said, "we think you have this one handled officer," got in the truck and drove off. We almost peed all over ourselves looking back at the cop dance around the puddle while trying to arrest this guy without having to touch him.

"SNIPER"

A call came in for a possible shooting in a warehouse district in the southwest end of Station 2's territory. When we arrived, we quickly realized the situation was more than just your standard shooting, if that even exists. Several police officers had taken up positions behind their vehicles and had their guns drawn and pointed toward the second floor of the warehouse.

I had my driver pull up away from the warehouse and ran to the first officer who was positioned well away from the building. Using binoculars from this vantage point, I could see three men on the ground by the loading dock. All three had gunshot wounds to the chest and were bleeding profusely. I asked the cop how long he had been there and if he had heard any gunfire. He said it had been eerily quiet for the five or six minutes he was on-scene but dispatch had advised that the shooter had not been contained and could still be in the area. In addition, one of the warehouse employees who escaped told them that at least 20 people were hiding inside the building, and one had fallen off a catwalk and was unconscious. The Special Weapons and Tactics (SWAT) squad had been called but they were on two separate calls and would be delayed. The term "active shooter" did not exist in the early 1990s and police tactics at that time were to secure the perimeters and wait for special response teams.

At this point, I had to make a decision. Based on the fact that there had been no gunfire for several minutes, I figured that the shooter had hit his intended victims and was probably long gone. All three victims were shot in the chest, so the shooter was probably both a good shot and left before the cops arrived or hit them all at close range. If we didn't go in, all three would probably die.

I quickly explained the situation to my crew and asked them if they were willing to go in to work the victims. Both of my crewmembers had about a year on the job and trusted me not to get them killed. They agreed, so we called for additional units, laid out a quick plan with the police, turned off the lights in the Rescue and I drove into the center of the u-shaped warehouse with my crew in the back.

All three victims were hit mid-chest and were in critical condition. We each took a victim and by the time the second rescue arrived, all three were immobilized on backboards and intravenous lines started. We loaded the most critical patient and headed for the JMH Trauma Center. I knew that if we were going to be shot at, this was the time. We had one of the shooter's intended victims and if he was here, he might try to finish him off and us as well. The cops had our backs and made sure we got out safely.

Thankfully, nothing happened. We got the patient to the trauma center and headed back to the scene for possible additional patients. When we arrived again, the warehouse had been emptied and the victim who had fallen turned out to have minor injuries. However, as we found out later, the shooter was not only still on the scene, but had actually led our Battalion Chief to the injured man inside the warehouse.

He apparently was angry that he had been passed over for a class that would have meant a possible promotion, so he shot the three victims as they returned from class. Two of them, including the victim we transported survived. Incredibly, this was not the killer's first offense. He had "accidently" killed his girlfriend several years before and served time in prison. He was captured a few days later in another part of the state.

"HOW TO JUMP A CALL"

One of things I found to be different in the busier areas of the County was that most of the firefighters, especially the officers, constantly monitored the radio. Part of it was the pride in responding to the call as quickly as possible, and part was the ability to jump calls in other territories. At the time, Miami-Dade had four frequencies: North, Central, South and Tactical. Stations 2 and 7 were on Central, but Station 7 was near the border of where Central and North frequencies were split. Station 26 was the next nearest station to the north of 7 and at the time, assigned to the North District and frequency. The Station 7 regulars had an unwritten rule and would keep one of the handheld radios on North and the truck radio on Central when we were on the road. Station 2 would also monitor North in a similar manner but was a little further away for jumping calls in the North District. While we were in the stations, most if not all of the officers would keep their handheld radios on to get that 30-60 second jump on a call. Both Rescue 2 and 7 bought scanners from Radio Shack (seriously!) to be able to monitor the local Miami-Dade Police Department (MDPD) frequencies. On a regular basis, we would actually notify our dispatchers that we were responding to a call with MDPD and would advise when we had additional information, such as an address, number of victims, etc. Dispatch got used to it, and when we stated "Rescue 2" or "Rescue 7", most of the dispatchers would simply ask, what do you have? The last thing we did on the trucks as far as communications was to install a stereo with a cassette deck (again, remember those?) that would shut down when the call came in and the microphone was keyed. The stereo would physically have to be turned back on when the exchange with the dispatcher was completed.

As I stated, most of the busier units across the County did pretty much the same thing. Occasionally, we would transport a patient to one of the hospitals in the north end of the County. When returning to our territory, we made a habit of rolling through Station 11's territory in what used to be called Carol City but is now part of Miami Gardens. The 11's were also busy units, and we all got along great, but there was always that friendly competition that bordered on maniacal when it came to running the most calls. After dropping a patient off and coming back through 11's territory, we saw three MDPD patrol cars fly by with emergency lights and sirens. I told my driver to follow them, and we flipped our lights on. They turned north on 27th Avenue and blew past Station 11. The Captain happened to be standing outside and saw us. I waved to him and smiled and he ran back inside the station. I told my crew, "Listen, they're going to ask for our location", and about 30 seconds later, the dispatcher comes on the air and asks, "Rescue 2, what's your QTH" (location)? I answered, "Northbound on 27th Avenue at 213th Street", which was way out of our territory. "We were flagged down by MDPD and told to follow." A few seconds later, we heard, "QSL (acknowledged), advise." When we cleared the call and got back to our house, 11's Captain called, jokingly cussing me out and said he knew we were jumping his calls but would do the same if he got the chance.

"HURRICANE ANDREW"

In 1992, the southern end of Miami-Dade County experienced what was at the time, the worst natural disaster in the nation's history. Until Hurricane Katrina made landfall, Hurricane Andrew was the costliest storm in history at 26 billion dollars (NWS, 2005). Andrew was the first and only named storm of the Atlantic hurricane season and developed almost three months into the season which was a rarity. Andrew's winds were originally thought to be a sustained 145 miles per hour making it a Category 4 storm, but a decade later, experts reviewed the data and determined the storm to have sustained winds of 165 with gusts over 200 mph. This made it then the third most powerful hurricane to make landfall in the United States, behind Hurricane Camille in 1969, and the unnamed storm in 1935 that hit Florida. 300 square miles were devastated, including homes and businesses, schools, hospitals and other residential healthcare facilities. Traffic signs, signals, and power lines were gone and water mains were severely damaged or completely out of commission. At the height of the storm, almost 1.5 million people lost electricity and another 150,000 were without telephone service. The Homestead Air Reserve Base, an economic engine supporting the area took a direct hit with most of the buildings on the base severely damaged or rendered totally unusable. A storm surge of up to 17 feet was measured at Burger King's International Headquarters in southern Miami-Dade County, and multiple neighboring single-story buildings were for all practical purposes washed away.

One of many homes devasted after Hurricane Andrew. This one belonged to a Miami-Dade County firefighter.

Even before the storm had subsided, fire crews were out in the community, assisting where they could. As members of the public began to realize the storm had finally passed, the number of calls began to increase exponentially. Landmarks were gone and every street looked the same, making it nearly impossible to find addresses, or to find the homes of our brother and sister firefighters and their families who lived in South Dade but had not reported in. We had personnel on the job that literally had not seen their families for days and were unsure if they had survived yet they continued to care for strangers who had suffered through the same destructive forces. This was long before cell phones were commonplace and finding specific locations using GPS coordinates was unheard of.

For the next week or two, our call volume was at least ten times the norm and seemed that it would never level off. For close to a month, we had to hold calls and respond on a priority basis; something Miami-Dade Fire Rescue had never done before. At one point we had as many as 300-400 calls holding. More often than not, when a rescue or suppression crew was dispatched to one call, they would encounter three or four citizens who flagged them down for medical issues, minor injuries, roads blocked with downed trees, or a multitude of other reasons.

In the aftermath, hundreds of local, state, and federal agencies as well as multiple private sector organizations came forward to help. Every little bit helped: essentials such as food and shelter, and the niceties that we take for granted such as electricity and hot water were gone. For weeks, dozens of firefighters would drive to a makeshift logistics center after their 24-hour shift was completed and pick up supplies provided by International Association of Firefighters (IAFF) Local 1403. These included necessities such as water, diapers, canned food, batteries, and roofing materials initially set aside for firefighters in need, but without a second thought shared with anyone else who needed them. Residents formed lines a half-mile long to get a gallon of water, a bag of ice, or field rations provided by the military called MREs (meals ready to eat). For those directly affected by the storm, it seemed like there was no end in sight.

Although hundreds of firefighters from across the country showed up to help, many came unannounced and unprepared. In addition, some utilized the "10" codes in their hometowns and had difficulty understanding the "Q" codes used in Miami-Dade County at that time. Using that incident as a catalyst, most agencies over the past two decades have gone to or are in the process of going to what is called clear text. Clear text is a message or data that is provided in a form that is immediately understandable to another person or persons without having to process it further. In order to be able to communicate effectively with personnel from other areas, the decision was made to go to clear text and speak as if we were simply holding a conversation.

As I said, many showed up with good intentions but totally unprepared. They had no food or water or a place to stay. Housing these volunteers was no easy task. Any hotel or motel room not destroyed or rendered uninhabitable by the storm was taken over by federal, state, and local officials, various contractors, faith-based, and other volunteer organizations. To accommodate the hundreds of volunteer firefighters, we doubled and tripled up in every fire station with people sleeping in shifts, on the floor, in the vehicles, or any other available open spot. Food and water was shared with our impromptu guests.

Regular crews were split up to ensure there would be a local firefighter on every unit who knew the area. I had a firefighter from South Carolina and one from Missouri assigned to me. One of the calls that we ran on was near the Caleb Center, a local community action and human services center that provided emergency food and shelter and general assistance in this particular lower socio-economic area. The kid from South Carolina was obviously not used to working in a predominantly Black neighborhood. This became apparent when we got out of the truck and out of probably close to 1,000 people, the three of us were the only white folks as far as the eye could see. Every time I took a step, the South Carolina firefighter was in my shadow or bumping into my back. Finally, one of the Black MDPD officers who I had known for years saw what was happening and told the kid something to the effect of "Man, relax, it's cool. Nothing's going to happen to you." He looked at me and we both smiled. The kid apologized and said that the town he was from only had about 500 residents and very few were Black. Welcome to the big city, kid.

We ran on multiple appliance fires, many starting in refrigerators.

For some, recovering from the devastation incurred by Hurricane Andrew lasted for months while others literally took several years. Hundreds of thousands of South Florida residents became homeless; over 25,000 homes were destroyed and an additional 100,000 were damaged. Many of the 1.5 million affected were without power for up to six months. When power did come back on in homes and businesses in the areas not completely leveled by the hurricane, power surges caused an abnormally large number of fires. Appliances without surge protectors were the biggest offenders, but the most unusual thing was the amount of fires stating inside refrigerators. Most of those fires probably started due to the loss of cooling inside the appliance and moisture from containers, the refrigerators themselves contacting electrical components or a heat-emitting element being exposed to combustible materials. For several shifts after returning to work, we ran dozens of fire-related calls each day. The irony was that there were many people who initially made it through the one of the worst storms in modern history only to lose everything in a fire indirectly caused by that same storm.

Over the next three or four months, things slowly started to return to normal, although much of the South Dade area and Homestead in particular didn't see signs of recovery for almost 20 years. Although the hurricane had a major economic impact on the County and caused significant environmental damage, life went on. Makeshift schools opened, people found alternate means of transportation to get to work, and some of the residents started to rebuild their homes and their lives.

At the time, our hurricane policy was considered the gold standard and emulated by most fire departments in South Florida. After Andrew, it was essentially tossed in the trash and rewritten. We thought we knew how to prepare for and recover from a hurricane, but we had never dealt with a Category 5 storm, the first to hit the mainland in 23 years.

"EAT OR BE EATEN"

In busy houses, we had what we considered the pack mentality. Either you were one of the hyenas, or you became the quarry in the hunt. There was nothing malicious about this predator/prey mindset. It kept everyone on his or her toes and made the day go by that much faster. In most houses, and actually in most departments, the newly assigned firefighters or probationary employees (recruits, rookies, probies) would be asked what he or she didn't like about the house or department, or what changes should be made and to write in on the blackboard. Most would pick up on this rather quickly, say everything was perfect and continue with their assignments, but some would always write something on the board to give us ammunition for the day. Of course, from that point on, we made sure we did whatever that firefighter said annoyed him.

Another basic rule in busier firehouses was that if you weren't a worker, we didn't like you, and if we didn't like you, we didn't socialize with you. Actually, it was more of a defense mechanism, as lazy or incompetent individuals have a tendency to complain the loudest about the pettiest of problems. If you were picked on, you were considered part of the group and accepted. Those who passed through and didn't appreciate our sense of humor were not subject to it, but generally left within a few months because the workload was too much for them.

"ROOKIE'S INTRODUCTION TO STATION LIFE"

Recruits are at times easier to train than seasoned firefighters. When trying to introduce new methods of accomplishing a task or new tactics, the standard reply from many who have been on the job for multiple years seems to be, "why do we have to learn a new way of doing things? It's worked well for us and we see no reason to change now."

The fire service has evolved over the years and will continue to do so; not necessarily by choice, but by necessity. Emergency Medical Services (EMS) and Air Rescue were each introduced in the 1960s, Hazardous Materials response in the 1970s, Water Response and Technical Rescue (TRT) in the 1980s, and in the 2000s, Terrorism Response.

Another training issue that periodically pops up are those probationary firefighters who want to do it all and do it now. They don't understand that not only do you have to crawl before you walk; you also have to mop the floors and clean the toilets before you go on a life-saving mission with Urban Search and Rescue (US&R) or perform a pick-off as a member of Technical Rescue (TRT) (see the chapter, "But I Want to be a Hero").

To that end, in the early 1990s Manny Morales and I developed a simple set of daily rules for probationary firefighters to follow when assigned to Station 2 or 7 "A" shift. They were called Rookie Rules or to be more politically correct, Station Etiquette for Probationary Firefighters. They were posted on the wall and every probationary firefighter would be provided with a copy and directed to read them, write them down, or carry it with them. As time went on, I added segments regarding cell phone use while on-duty:

Arrival:

- Arrive 30 minutes prior to the start of your shift if possible, no later than 15 minutes before (not mandatory, but highly recommended).
- Don't be a minute man (someone who shows up one minute before the start of the shift).
- Be ready to run a call as soon as you get to the station. This means you put your gear on the truck as soon as you arrive and are ready to go.
- Remember: the firefighter you are replacing wants to leave as soon as his/her shift is over, and you would like someone to do that for you.
- If the off-going firefighter must run a call 15 minutes before the end of shift, he/she may not return to the station until an hour or more afterward.
- This may affect more than just that firefighter; he or she may be replacing another firefighter at another station.
- Report to your assigned station clean-shaven and in full uniform even if you are working overtime.

- Check every compartment in every apparatus in thestation including the Battalion Chief's vehicle after you check the truck you are assigned to. Whether assigned to the Rescue or Suppression, you may be instructed to locate equipment from the other apparatus on a call.

Introductions:

- Introduce yourself to the first uniformed employee you see, and if you don't already know, ask who your officer is and which apparatus you are assigned to.
- Introduce yourself to:
- Your officer.
- Your crew.
- The officer and crew of the other apparatus in the station.
- All other uniform personnel in the station, whether on-duty or not.
- Five minutes after you introduce yourself, most of the people will not remember your name. If you don't bother to introduce yourself, they'll all remember you!

Assignments:

- After all the apparatus have been checked, ask your officer for your station assignments.
- When completed, ask your officer if there is anything else for you to do.
- You are the rookie; your job is to answer the telephone every time it rings.

- Identify yourself by station, rank and name, in that order. If the recall goes off, go immediately to your assigned apparatus unless directed otherwise.
- Learn the proper procedure for answering the radio but do not answer unless specifically instructed to do so by your officer.
- If the doorbell rings, answer it. Greet the public, take blood pressures; answer questions if you can, and if you can't, ask someone else! You don't know everything, so don't pretend to.
- When you have free time, ask questions, complete your modules and study, study, study.
- Do not take a nap while you are probation, even if someone tells you it is okay. They might be testing you.
- Unless you are on a special diet, be prepared to eat with the crews. Don't ask what they are cooking.
- If your diet is not medically prescribed, it would be smart to pay for the meal whether you eat it or not.
- Pay your kitty and don't be a kitty hound. The kitty is not there to provide you with three meals a day.

Overtime:

- If you are working overtime, immediately advise your OIC that you are a probationary firefighter. Do not pretend to be a seasoned veteran, as it could put you and your crew in danger.
- Be prepared to pay five dollars or bring a dessert.
- This is not a written rule, just a courtesy to your fellow fire-fighters. You are now making one and one-half times the normal pay rate for that shift and can well afford five dollars or the going rate.

- Lieutenants should pay $10, Captains $20, and Chief Fire Officers should buy dinner for the entire station.

Personal Time:

- If you are not busy running calls after completion of station assignments use your time wisely. Complete the assigned modules in your workbook, read articles from the Fire or Rescue journals supplied at each station, or recheck the equipment on the apparatus. Someone's life may depend upon it.
- Cell phones should be used for emergencies only.
- There is no other reason for you to use one while on the apparatus or on a call. You can tell your family and friends about your day or an exciting call when you get off-duty. Cell phones should be put in silent or vibration mode at the beginning of the shift. It's unprofessional, inappropriate, and annoying for one to start beeping or ringing while you're on a call.

Interaction with the Public:

- Do not perform personal errands on-duty unless absolutely necessary. Everyone has a cell phone camera and is looking to find fault with what you do and document it.
- Do not go into, park in front of, or give the perception that you are even interested in the contents of a gun, liquor, or cigar store. Remember, perception is the new reality.

- Do not high-five, hug, or shake hands with any other department members on a call, regardless of how long it's been since you've seen them.
- Remember bullets one and two, cameras and perception.
- Members of the public will rarely approach you with a complaint: they will go directly to the mayor, commissioner, council member or fire chief.
- Right or wrong, you still must justify your actions.
- When in public, look professional, act professional, think professional and be professional. Firefighters are no longer the good guys; many think you are overpaid and underworked.

A person's first impression of you is a lasting one. Your reputation, good or bad will precede you to every station in the County. MAKE SURE IT'S A GOOD ONE.

"THE PRATTVILLE BOYS"

It's easy to understand why EMT and Paramedic students as well as veteran firefighters from smaller urban, and many rural departments want to ride with busier companies to gain experience. Miami-Dade Fire Rescue's reputation is internationally renowned, with departments from all over North, Central, South America, and the Caribbean sending personnel to South Florida to train with and learn from some of the best in the business. Students come from as far away as Anchorage Alaska (think it's for the weather?), and Central and South Americans for the ability to converse in their native language.

Professional courtesy was extended to both domestic and international paramedic and/or firefighters from other departments, allowing them to stay at the firehouses, and many times in our own homes. Unfortunately, there is always one or two who abuse the privilege. Under the guise of completing a ride-along, a few decided to use the firehouse as a place to stay while vacationing in South Florida. After taking advantage of us for three years in a row, they were banned from visiting the stations or riding with the crews. They quickly became persona non-grata with neighboring departments across three counties.

As MDFR received hundreds of domestic and dozens of international requests to visit the stations each year, a standardized set of procedures were established to ensure that the visits were of an official nature. Documentation required included a copy of an Interpol background check if necessary, a certified copy of each applicant's birth certificate, a letter of responsibility from the head of the agency or organization identifying the official reason for the visit, and a good quality organization photo ID. Before anyone could visit, the documents were forwarded to the MDPD Homeland Security Bureau for processing before considering the request to visit.

The aircraft crashed and skidded across busy 72 Ave.

In 1997, two firefighters from Prattville, Alabama were approved to ride as observers on both Rescue 2 and Rescue 7 for three consecutive shifts. At the time, Prattville was a town of about 20,000 residents, and their Fire Department had about 50 members. They rode with the crews for up to 16 hours each shift and tried to get some sleep in between unless it was a significant call such as a trauma, fire, or major incident. They got very little rest in 72 hours but responded to a lifetime of calls in those three days. Their second call of the first day was the Fine Air Flight 101 crash. The aircraft lost power after takeoff from Miami International Airport, crashing onto a busy surface street and scattering cars and trucks. The three crewmembers and one security guard on board perished, and a motorist on the ground was killed. In all, over 100 response personnel were involved in the call. During the rest of their first day, they had a warehouse fire, two house fires, and a high-speed vehicular accident with a multi-trauma. The second day wasn't any slower. Around 25 or so calls, including a tanker truck that lost control and rolled over on U.S. 836, exploding into flames. By the time the third day was completed, all one of them could say with that distinct Southern drawl was "I seen more calls in three days than I seen in three years!"

Just after arrival on the tanker fire.

"NO CALLS AFTER MIDNIGHT"

The alert tones went off for a shooting; at least eight victims. The assignment initially consisted of Rescues 2 and 7, Squrt 2, Engine 7, and Battalion 5. Generally, on major traumas or fire responses, the dispatcher would advise how many calls they received for us to get a better feel for whether the call was real or questionable. In this case, it was a single call.

On a multiple casualty incident such as this one, the first arriving officer's responsibility was to size up the situation, estimate the number of victims and quickly determine the need for additional units. We arrived first and found nothing. No victims, witnesses, bystanders, blood stains, or bullets casings and slowed the other units down. I asked the dispatcher to give me any caller information she had. She was able to provide the address of the phone the call came from, a block away and to our surprise, we found a newly installed pay phone. We cancelled the incoming units and cleared the scene. An hour later, they dispatched us to another call in the same general area, this time for a building fire. Another pay phone, another false alarm. For the rest of the night, we advised the dispatchers that it would only be a single unit response to anything in that area and rotated units out of Station 2.

What we found out several days later was that the local phone service provider decided to install four pay phones in the Scott projects. I am sure this was done at the behest of one of the local politicians, but neither fire rescue or law enforcement authorities were consulted nor notified. Although we normally responded to one or two false alarms per shift, this increase greatly affected our ability to respond to real calls and several times, units from several miles away had to be dispatched while we were trying to determine if the call we were on was authentic.

Again, this was well before the widespread use of cell phones. Additionally, most people were unaware that there was no charge for calls made to 911 as well as dialing "0" to reach an operator. In addition to our normal complement of real calls, we totaled eight false alarm shooting and fire calls after midnight the first night, seven the second, and eight on the third night. Our next shift on-duty we waited to see what would happen. Just as expected, a few minutes after midnight, the first call came in; another false alarm. With police officers accompanying our crew, I went to the first pay phone and permanently "dismantled" the receiver and the wiring console. We went from phone to phone until all four phones were rendered inoperative. The next morning, I contacted a telephone company representative, gave him my name, rank and contact information and advised what I had done and why. There was a long pause on his end of the phone: he then apologized profusely and stated the phones would be removed that day.

"AMBULANCES ON STEROIDS"

As with most fire rescue organizations today, Miami-Dade Fire Rescue transport units are actually ambulances on steroids. Even then, in addition to almost being the equivalent of a rolling Intensive Care Unit, equipment carried on-board included but was not limited to turnout, or bunker gear, SCBAs, and SCUBA dive gear. Some of the busier units developed procedures for and carried rapid intervention equipment such as air chisels, reciprocating saws and extra air bottles, 20 years before the Rapid Intervention Team (RIT) concept became part of the system in Miami-Dade County.

As we saw a considerable number of trauma calls, especially shootings, Rescues 2 and 7 were regularly assigned to the presidential motorcades whenever the Commander-in-Chief came to town. As Miami and South Florida in general was a focal point prior to elections, we participated in as many as a dozen or more annual visits. During my time at Stations 2 and 7, we were assigned to motorcades for Presidents Reagan, Bush Sr., and Clinton on multiple occasions, as well as numerous visits by vice-presidents, heads of state, other high-level dignitaries, and those running for office who at times required a motorcade to their destination. We became friendly and on a first name basis with many of the Secret Service agents assigned to the Miami Division.

"BUT I WANT TO
BE A HERO"

Occasionally, the fire service ends up with individuals who are able to pass the written exam and background check, say all the right things at an oral interview, and pass the minimum standards test, but once in the field, are found to be obviously wrong for the job. Why does this happen? Firefighting is a team-oriented occupation, whether on the scene or in the firehouse. When you choose this profession, you also become part of a brotherhood that encompasses almost one-third of your adult lives.

A firefighter's probationary period normally lasted one year, and during that time, probation was split into four separate three-month segments. During each of those periods, the proby would be assigned to a primary supervisor who he or she would ride with, or if at another station, report in to at least once toward the end of each shift, and to discuss any major issues encountered during that shift. At the end of each shift, the officer-in-charge who directly oversaw the probationary employee was required to write a daily evaluation, which the employee would keep in a workbook. As with many departments, performance standards were subdivided into four categories; Unsatisfactory, Needs Improvement, Satisfactory, and Above Satisfactory. Probationary firefighters were required to maintain a minimum of

Satisfactory on a daily basis. The daily evaluations were compiled to establish a monthly evaluation, and at the end of each period, the rookie would receive another three-month assignment and different primary supervisor.

We had one of those rookies who didn't quite get it. He was initially assigned to one of the friendliest, most capable Lieutenants in the department who was well respected by his peers and his command-ing officers. When his first three-month evaluation period concluded, many of the rookie's daily ratings were graded Needs Improvement, including his last monthly evaluation. As is normally done, the officer who served as his primary supervisor called ahead to brief me on the individual. One of the most pressing issues was convincing him that his job consisted of not only responding to medical and fire calls, but also doing the menial work, such as taking trash to the dumpster, sweeping the bays, or cleaning the bathrooms. Everyone took his or her turn in the barrel and he was no different.

With little over three months on the job, all he could talk about was becoming a member of the Technical Rescue and the Urban Search and Rescue Teams. I repeatedly had to remind him to crawl before he walked, and walk before he ran, so to speak. His response was always, "Yes, Captain, I understand," but never seemed to appreci-ate what the others and I were trying to tell him.

One of his daily chores as the least senior of all personnel was to clean the toilets and urinals: not the most prestigious of tasks, but necessary nonetheless. Some of the other firefighters advised me that he wasn't cleaning the urinals or the rest of the bathroom as was required each shift. I decided to test him one morning by placing a crumpled, but clean paper towel on top of one of the urinals. Once everyone had completed their station duties, I asked the firefighter if he had completed his tasks. He replied that he had. I then asked him, "Including the bathroom? Are you sure?" He wasn't aware of it, but the other firefighters and officer in the room slowly turned and looked in our direction, knowing what was next to come. When supervisory personnel pointedly ask if one is sure about a response, it generally means that person is being given a way out and a chance to reconsider their response. Adamantly clinging to the initial reply only buries you further. In this case, he did just that.

I took him aside and stated bluntly that as far as I was concerned, that was his last chance. The department as a whole and I personally would not tolerate dishonesty on the part of a probationary employee let alone a veteran firefighter. He begged for one more chance to correct his behavior and said he would do whatever it took to keep his job.

For the remainder of the three-month period that I served as his primary supervisor, there were no more incidents. Training reassigned him at the six-month mark and he completed his probationary period without further issue. He apparently resigned from the department for unknown reasons a few years later.

"STUDENT CENTRAL"

In addition to international students, many of the local colleges and universities as well as vocational schools with EMT and/or Paramedic programs had agreements with Miami-Dade Fire Rescue for their students to complete their required ride-alongs. These agreements included stipulations as what their students could or could not do when riding with MDFR, hours of operation, codes of conduct, etc. In the almost 20 years spent in Battalion 5, I estimate that I supervised close to 1,800 students completing their ride time on Rescue 2 or Rescue 7. Most of the students were respectful, understood exactly why they were there, and were able to comply with both their school policies and our departmental rules.

Regrettably, there's always one or two who have difficulty following the rules. The first that comes to mind was a student from one of the local colleges. He arrived at the station for his ride time at 07:58 hours, two minutes before his 08:00-shift started. That was the first strike. When you're one of 15,000-20,000 people vying for 300 jobs, you don't want to start off by making a bad impression with those for whom you want to work. His second mistake was that he wore a white button-down shirt as per his school dress code, but also wore a t-shirt underneath imprinted with a logo flaunting, 'Beer, it's what's for dinner" with a large stein in the center. He was told in uncertain terms to immediately remove the shirt. He wasn't pleased, but he removed it as directed. His third and final mistake as far as we were concerned, was to return to Station 2 several weeks later on another shift, wearing the same banned tee under his white collared shirt. He assumed that since I was not working, the on-duty officer wouldn't know that he had been told earlier to dress appropriately.

As I said before, your reputation precedes you. We may not call ahead to the next firehouse about a student, but we certainly discuss their attitudes, interaction, and professionalism in-house from shift to shift. He was sent home, the school was notified, and he was dismissed from the program.

The second incident that made an impact was a student who followed directives until it came to a relatively serious situation that could have put his life in danger. A call came in for a fire in a mobile home park. As we arrived, we were advised by police that there was gunfire coming from the trailer that was burning. I ordered the student to stay with the truck at the entrance of the trailer park while we made our way toward the scene. As we approached, I could see around the corner of a mobile home across from the one on fire. Visible flames were shooting out two windows and a man waving a revolver was hanging out a third window. As I turned to tell my crew to standby, I saw the student standing behind them, peering around the corner. I yelled at him to get back to the truck immediately and told one of my crew to escort him there. As Engine 7 arrived, one of the police officers risked his life by sneaking up on the gunman, grabbed his gun hand and yanked him through the open window. A second officer jumped in and both pulled him to safety. We then moved in to knock down the fire.

Once the fire was put out, I returned to our truck where the firefighter was babysitting the EMT student. After chewing him a new one for disobeying orders and putting himself and our crew at risk, I put our Rescue out of service until we could deposit him back at the station and send him home. His evaluation reflected his actions, but it's unknown if the school took additional action against him. We never saw him again.

ADDITIONAL PHOTOS

With my partner Gene after a house fire.

Duke Adkinson and I are posing in front of the "Hooker's Cove" sign. A citizen was making
a statement about the neighborhood: the sign was gone the next day.

Graduating class # 57, 1984; I'm in the center, back. row.

Getting ready to go in a ship's hold on a confined space drill.

Listening to two of the best during the World Trade Center response:
Mike Nugent from FL TF-2 and Al Perry from FL TF-1.

Graduating from the confined space rescue course.

Old Firehouse 7: a tight fit on either side. Engine 7's bay was on the east side and just as bad.

I guess it was meant to be: here I am at about three-years old in my first fire truck.

Smoking cigars behind Firehouse 2, Battalion 5 style.

Joe Starling and me with one of the regulars.

Coming out of the water after a search.

Sort of goes without saying...

Our squad and one of the others were getting ready to come home after 9/11.

The first chance to call home after responding to the World Trade Center attack.

The new Firehouse 7: three times as big and   just as busy.

The dorm in old Firehouse 7. You had to turn sideways to get past the first two bunks.

My first ID; darker hair, mustache, sunglasses?

Taking a break during the construction of a Habitat for Humanity home:
what an honor to participate and an opportunity to help others.
Once again, I'm in the back row, just right of center
with the tilted hat and sunglasses.

"BLACK TOWER AND WHITE ZINFANDEL"

After I was promoted to Lieutenant, I was able to get the bid at Station 7 without much of an effort. As I've said, if you want to work in a busy house, you'll find a way. Two of the best firefighter-paramedics that I ever worked with also bid in at Station 7 soon after that. Joe Sollecito, a stocky Italian-American with an attitude that fit in perfectly with the mindset of the guys in Battalion 5, and Robert Flintroy, a big Black guy who liked to tell everybody how quick he was on his feet. He actually moved pretty well for a 280-pounder. His nickname was "Cookie Monster" because he loved to bake cookies…, and eat…, and eat…, and eat. Bobby always said that the presentation itself was more important than actually eating, but he could put away the groceries. He was a great guy and a great cook, but he used every pot and pan in the station on his cook day, and it took us hours to clean the grease off the floor, walls, and ceiling. Joe on the other hand didn't like to cook. He used the stove at his house for storage: if he wasn't on-duty, he went to a restaurant.

Joe was also the Department's unofficial financial counselor. He was heavily into the stock market and did extensive research on any stock he looked into buying. He knew most of the CEO's of the companies he dealt with by name, and they knew him. He was so adept at picking stocks that at one point he was actually interviewed by the Securities and Exchange Commission for possible insider trading. They too were impressed with his research techniques and dropped the investigation.

As I said, I couldn't ask for better partners in Joe and Bobby. If either one went into a shooting call ahead of me or called for a trauma alert, I never asked what we had, I just immediately forwarded the information to our dispatcher.

Both of them had a reputation outside the station as being whiners. They really weren't, but since we liked to pick on our friends every chance we got, we played along with the reputations; therefore, they were nicknamed Black Tower and White Zinfandel; two wines for two whiners. They appreciated the humor and played it up every chance they got. Both are still my good friends to this day.

"A FRIEND SURVIVES; AND SURVIVES; AND SURVIVES"

A few additional words about Manny Morales: In the mid-90's Manny had gone to training as a change of pace. So did several other outstanding firefighters, including Steve Hondares and Cesar Fabal. One weekday morning, Manny was crossing a busy intersection near headquarters to have a key made at a hardware store. Before he made it halfway across the street, he was hit by a car whose driver didn't see him in the crosswalk. The impact threw him across the hood and he crumpled in the street like a rag doll. By the Grace of God, Steve and Cesar were on the scene in seconds, secured his airway, stabilized his cervical spine, and kept him alive until the nearest rescue could arrive. In extremely critical condition, he was transported to the trauma center where he was put on life support. There was no question that their actions had saved his life, but for weeks, we didn't know if he'd live or die. His head swelled to twice its original size, and he sustained a fractured skull, arm, and leg, and multiple internal injuries.

We tried our best to be there for his wife and children, but it was hard to put on a front when you thought one of your brothers was going to die. When he eventually got past the most critical point to where he would be able to survive, the neurosurgeons told us he would probably be brain-damaged. At this point, we actually had to shift gears and start to think of how we were going to take care of him long-term. More importantly, we had to be there for his kids.

As the days grew into weeks, they started noticing more and more positive physical responses, such as moving his fingers or toes on command. As the weeks turned into months, his lucidity began to return. Even though he was still confined to a wheelchair, he was showing signs of the old Manny coming through. He started to become obnoxious and sarcastic; a very good sign! The neurosurgeons were shocked, calling it nothing short of a miracle. His faculties began to come back and as he started to become more aware of his surroundings, he would say that if I was really his friend, I'd help him escape from the hospital. Each time I'd refuse, saying that the hospital was the best place for him until he recovered. He'd threaten me, curse at me, and say I wasn't a real friend or I'd get him out of there. Man, was I happy! Over the next few months, he continued to improve, first by slowly getting out of the wheelchair and using a walker. Eventually, he was able to walk without mechanical assistance although he walked with a pronounced limp. We told him that if we knew he was going to survive, we would have written our names on his chest with indelible ink instead of putting them in his visitor's log.

A little over a year after he was written off for dead or brain-damaged, he came back to Operations. We had a relatively easy shift, but around 03:00 hours, a call came in for a car fire and both Engine and Rescue 7 responded. When we arrived, we helped pull a jump line, but then we stood back and watched him knock down the fire on his own. When it was over, we all started applauding. At that moment, Manny was the happiest firefighter in the world.

About two years later after Manny had been promoted to Lieutenant, his crew responded to a warehouse fire in 2's territory. At some time while fighting the fire, he started getting cold and clammy and literally had to be carried out by his crew. It turned out he had a blockage in the coronary arteries that led to a small heart attack. Once again, he was out with a serious life-threatening injury.

Unbelievably, Manny was back in Operations within the year. He was one of the most stubborn people I have ever known. This guy had not one, but two life-threatening incidents that most people would have simply taken the disability money and run. Truthfully though, I expected no less from this man.

Unfortunately, because of the multiple blood transfusions he received in emergency surgery after he was hit by the car, Manny eventually contracted Hepatitis C and died shortly after retirement. His legacy lives on through his son Chris who's made his own mark in the department. Manny would be proud.

"MOTORCYCLE DOWN"

I can clearly remember one call that occurred in 1994 that stood out for several reasons. We were clearing from a run and heard a call go out on the police scanner. Motorcycle accident, multiple patients, unknown injuries. It was out of our territory but as soon as we caught the address, we were in route giving us at least a one-minute jump on any other responding units. When we arrived, we found a motorcyclist who had run into the passenger side of a car that made a U-turn right in front of him. According to witnesses, the biker never had a chance to avoid the accident. His girlfriend was ejected off the back of the bike and landed about 30 feet away, crumpled in a heap. An engine crew arrived a few seconds later and we directed them to her position while we went to work on the cyclist. It was obvious that his right femur (long bone in the thigh) was fractured, as that leg was slightly shorter than the left and turned outward, typical signs associated with that type of break. His hip also appeared to be dislocated as the leg was twisted at almost a right angle away from his body. To make matters worse, he had no pedal (top of the foot or on the ankle) pulses or feeling and was clearly a candidate to lose the leg.

Our medical procedures prohibited us from reducing (repositioning the bone) dislocations or fractures, but he was conscious and in tremendous pain. Although I knew I was violating policy, I made the decision to reduce the dislocation for several reasons: the position was such that it would have been extremely difficult to transport him by ground or air, and in all probability, the lack of blood flow might result in his losing the leg. Almost as soon as this was done, you could see that his level of pain had been significantly reduced. His pulses returned: we put him in a traction splint that aligned the leg and separated the bone ends, also relieving the pain, and transported him to the trauma center.

Now why was this call meaningful to me? About two weeks before this accident, I had decided to buy a new Harley Davidson Fatboy. When I saw that the motorcycle in the accident was identical to the Harley I wanted, it hit home. After the call was over, I learned that the man operating the bike was 42 years old, my age at the time. I also realized that if that was me, I wouldn't be able to continue working or support my family. It's one thing to be involved in a wreck in a vehicle with four wheels, but another to lose control and most certainly hit the pavement hard on a two-wheeler. Another noteworthy reason: about five shifts later, nurses at the trauma center told me that my patient worked for the City of Miami and was a brother firefighter. Everything happens for a reason, and this was one more thing telling me to forget about buying a bike.

Almost three years after the accident, there was a knock on the door at Station 7. One of my crew answered it and said someone was looking for me. When I went to the door, a guy in a City of Miami firefighter uniform said, "You're a hard man to find. I've been looking for you for three years to say thanks; you saved my life, my leg and my job." We both came close to losing our composure and after multiple bro-hugs, sat down to talk. After multiple surgeries, he ended up only losing a toe on his right foot. He now walked with a slight limp but was able to go back to work after almost a year in the hospital and rehabilitation. His girlfriend also survived the wreck and Mark (the firefighter) finished out his career as an inspector.

I saw him several more times, unfortunately mostly at firefighter funerals. He retired a year before I did and I haven't seen him since. I hope he's doing well.

"LIEUTENANT WHO...?"

We had a great rapport with the police officers assigned to our district, to the point that when we saw one of them on a traffic stop at night, we'd pull over and wait until a backup unit arrived, they cleared the scene or waved us off. They would also feel comfortable enough to come into our station and hang up their gun belts in the back room while they were on break. As we considered them family, we used to pick on them mercilessly. For years, we would change our names for any of the new cops in the territory. A favorite was adding "mouse" to the end of your name, such as Adkinsonmouse, or Palestrantmouse.

The veteran police officers who had been fooled like everyone else obviously wanted to pay it forward, so of course they wanted their rookies to look foolish too and never gave us up. Some additional names we used were related to Star Trek characters and depended on the officer's rank. The Lieutenant was Worf, and the Captains were of course, Kirk, and then Picard. When this became incredibly easy, we started with names like Clouseau. When a police officer asked if I were a Lieutenant or Captain, I'd tell him I just transferred from Inspections, and I was still officially an Inspector. Therefore, I was Inspector Clouseau from the Pink Panther movies.

They'd never look at our nametags and had no reason to think we'd lie to them, so they wrote anything we gave them. Eventually, Sollecito, Flintroy and I started using new names. I became Constantine Nicopapadoupoulous, Flintroy was Pyotr Wasikosiloscowitz, and Sollecito was Joe Fu. The cops would try to write these names on small pocket-sized notebooks and almost took up the whole page before they were finished. Spelling was a near impossibility for most of the officers, but Sollecito would look them in the eye and tell them his name was spelled F-U. We became adept at pronouncing and spelling these names, and eventually most of the cops called us by those names whenever they saw us. If it were a serious call, or one that might have had implications of going to court for any reason, we would give our real names.

"IT WASN'T THEIR TIME"

According to witnesses and a police report, a 15-year-old girl was approached by an unknown adult just a few yards from her home while walking home from school one day. The individual grabbed the girl and threw her into his car, but during the scuffle, the girl screamed and her older brother and father who happened to be in their front yard heard the commotion. They saw her forced into the kidnapper's vehicle, but it was too far away to catch him on foot. They quickly jumped into their car to try to stop him, but he had already taken off. Neighbors who heard the commotion called 911 but the father and brother were already in pursuit. As the kidnapper realized he was being chased, he began to shoot at his pursuers. Most of the bullets were wild, but one went through the windshield between the father and brother and struck the steering wheel.

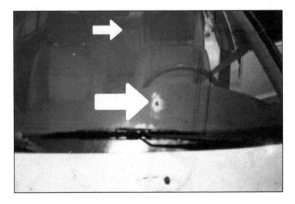

The bullet ricocheted off the steering wheel and penetrated the back seat (arrows).

Somehow, the projectile missed both family members and lodged in the back seat. At approximately the same time, the would-be kidnapper lost control and went over a curb, almost rolling over and sliding to a stop. Neither the girl nor the kidnapper was injured in the accident, but by the time police arrived a minute or so later, the assailant had sustained multiple broken bones, lacerations and bruises, courtesy of the brother and father. The kidnapper was taken to Ward "D", the police holding area at Jackson Hospital, and thankfully, the young lady went home safe and sound thanks to the heroics of her father and brother.

"SENIORITY PAYS"

It was the middle of summer, hot and humid the way we like it in South Florida. A call came in as woman with difficulty breathing at a gas station. We were clearing from another call, and Squrt 2 was closer and responded with us, arriving about a minute before we did. When we got there, all I saw were blank stares on everyone's faces. Sort of like, we know what we have to do, but how do we take the first step?

I saw, to be kind, a heavyset woman well over 400 lbs. in a very small car with two Chihuahuas. Unfortunately, the woman was trying to get home because she had to engage in an emergency act of defecation and didn't quite make it. Her Toyota died a few blocks from home, and she started hyperventilating due to the impending situation. She had let loose with a massive bowel movement that escaped the Omar the Tentmaker designer dress she was wearing, and now the contents of her lower intestines decorated the entire front seat, most of the back seat, the dashboard, windshield, and side windows. Apparently, both Chihuahuas, excited by the commotion, had repeatedly run through the fecal matter and now looked like small light brown Dalmatians with dark brown spots. Everywhere they stepped, they tracked the crap, and they were now standing on their hind legs, looking like they were desperately trying to breathe out the partially opened driver's side window.

It seems that the woman was sitting in the car for some time before a Good Samaritan with blunted olfactory receptors called 911. The odor was absolutely overpowering. I was standing upwind at least two feet away and could still get a good whiff of the event at hand. As I wondered what she had eaten before that fateful trip, I immediately took charge and thought, "This is where seniority has its advantages!"

I directed three of the most seniority-challenged firefighters to put on their bunker (turnout) gear (SCBA optional), get into the car with the woman and get her out where we (they) could fully examine her. Once this phase of the evolution was completed, we placed her on the stretcher. Her blood pressure was somewhat elevated, so we recommended that she go to the hospital. She refused to go unless her dogs were taken care of, so I turned them over to a police officer that I had known since high school. "Dean, I put these animals in your capable hands, but make sure you wear gloves!" After some well-chosen words to me in private, Dean told the woman he would ensure that her dogs would be taken home by a neighbor bathed and disinfected. The woman agreed to let us transport her to the hospital but how they got the car home was another story.

While in route to the hospital, we turned on every fan and opened every vent in the truck. Both of my crewmembers wore dust masks (before high-efficiency particulate absorption or Hepa filters were available) and I, sitting at her head with the fans and A/C vents at my back, chose to mouth-breathe. Needless to say, the hospital personnel were less than pleased, but put her in an isolation unit until they could clean her up.

"WHY WE GOT PAID THE BIG BUCKS"

Early one afternoon in late November, a call came in for a mobile home fire. Both units from Station 2 and Station 7 responded as well as several others in the immediate area. While in route, we were advised of persons trapped. With cooler weather, smoke has a tendency to lay low and is not visible until you're almost on top of it. As we turned the corner, we could see heavy smoke and flame coming out of the south end of the trailer. The wind was blowing north at about 15-20 knots and the fire was quickly working toward the opposite end of the trailer, which we believed to be the bedroom. We immediately made it a Code 1, which was at the time, our terminology for a working fire.

There was a van in front of the mobile home and civilians were screaming that two people were still inside, one wheelchair-bound. Rescue 2 and Engine 7 arrived simultaneously, and both crews attempted to make entry through the only entrance that was on the southwest side of the trailer. Typically, in underprivileged neighborhoods, the secondary entrance to these trailers in mobile home parks is boarded shut for security purposes. This was no different; as Squrt 2 and Rescue 7 arrived, they began to try to tear off the screwed-down plywood and to make entry through the window at the north end of the trailer. Meanwhile the fire was beating us back. For every two feet forward, we were pushed one foot back. Eventually we made some headway, but the fire flashed after one of the firefighters opened an interior door. After several minutes, we made our way to the bedroom, which had been almost consumed by the flames.

You should understand something about firefighters. Deep down, we know that in many situations, there is little or no chance for victims to survive, or worse, there's no one in the structure and we're putting our lives at risk because somebody thinks someone may be in there, or think they heard someone screaming. It doesn't matter. The bottom line is that's what our job entails and why we are paid the big bucks: to go into burning buildings while everyone else is running out and to take chances when those only chances are slim and none.

Pat Alvarado is on the left. You can see where he covered the skin flap on his right forearm with a dressing and went right back to work.

In this particular case, it was just that: the occupants had been gone for hours and a Good Samaritan just wanted us to make sure they had not come home early. For our efforts, three of us suffered burns. While crawling down the hallway, my protective hood snagged on something and snapped away from my face for a split-second resulting in second-degree burns. Capt. Gary Pilger also received minor second-degree burns on his forehead where the metal band was pressed into the rubber seal on his facemask, and F/F Pat Alvarado received serious second-degree burns on both wrists when the fire flashed and he had to bail out a small bathroom window. When he dove out the window, his bunker coat caught on the frame and pulled both wrist snaps free and away from his gloves. When he got out of the trailer, he did not even notice his injuries until one of the other firefighters saw him pulling hose with skin flaps hanging from both arms. He had them cover the flaps with gauze dressings and went right back to work. He has healed completely since that fire and has been promoted to Lieutenant. Our injuries were relatively minor: the burns were dressed and we went back to work. We marked as a lesson learned but it certainly didn't change the way we fought fires.

"FAITHFUL DOG"

Early one weekend morning, a call came in from a lawn service employee for a female down inside a house. As we responded, additional information was transmitted advising that family members had not heard from or spoken to the elderly woman for several days. Generally, when this happens, it means that the individual has most likely passed away. In this particular case, we arrived to find the woman with the lower part of her body partially visible through open jalousies windows. Jalousies were a series of roughly six-inch glass panes on an exterior door and were popular in Florida in the 1960's to control the amount of light or air passing through.

After unsuccessfully attempting to make verbal contact with woman, I decided to send one of my crew, Olga Warner, through a window to check on her status. There was some discussion as to whether it was safe to enter as the house was covered with dog feces. As the feces appeared to come from one or more small dogs, we felt there was minimal danger to Olga and since she was the smallest of the three of us, assisted her through the window. She made her way to the kitchen area where the body was, and unlocked the door to let us in. At that point, we realized that this woman had passed away several days ago. There was no smell as a fan was on and blowing constantly toward the slightly open jalousies.

What was different about this call was the fact that a good portion of her face was missing; it appeared that the puppy in the house had run out of food and began to lick his owner's face. When the tissue began to come off with the persistent licking, the pup started to chew on the remaining flesh. It's normal for a canine in the wild to return to the feral state and in this particular case, the environment remained in an urban setting, ergo the house. Most of her face was stripped off down to the bone (I declined to add the photo to preserve her dignity). We called police for the medical examiner to retrieve the body, and Animal Services to pick up the dog.

When the Animal Services representative arrived, the officer picked up the pup and held him close to comfort him while returning to his truck. I asked what they do with a dog in a case such as this. As he hadn't seen the deceased, he had a puzzled look on his face. Then I asked, "can you offer them for adoption after they've eaten human flesh?" He turned white and suddenly held the dog out at arm's length. He immediately muzzled the dog as if it were a four-legged Hannibal Lecter from Silence of the Lambs. I kept my poise and slowly walked away.

"LIE DETECTOR? WHAT LIE DETECTOR?"

A call came in for a house fire: nothing major, just some light smoke coming from one of the closets in a bedroom. Normally, closets in bedrooms don't have electrical outlets, aren't used to store flammable liquids, or are likely sites for ignition sources. They are however, a favorite place for children to play with matches. We contained it in just a few minutes and walked outside to where the police had two ten-year-old boys in their care. As usual, the parents weren't home and the police had to conduct an investigation unless one or both of the kids confessed. One of the officers told me that they were pretty sure that the kids had started the fire but would not own up to it. They were street-wise and had no intentions on ratting on each other.

I asked the officers to bring one of the kids to the back of the rescue and to leave the door open just enough to where the other boy could see what was going on. We hooked up the defibrillator monitor leads to the kid and told him it was a lie detector and we would ask him a few questions. Then we slowly closed the back door to the rescue while the other kid was craning his neck to see what was going on. We told the boy in the truck that every time he told the truth, we would know by the squiggly lines on the monitor, and if he lied, an alarm would go off. What we didn't tell him was that whenever we asked a question that we thought he was less than truthful, we would set off the audible alarm. We did that two or three times; enough to have the kid start to get wide-eyed. We unhooked him, led him to the back door and brought him out.

As we were bringing the second ten-year-old in, he started screaming, "It wasn't me! It wasn't me! Darrell did it! He was playing with matches in Grandma's closet!" The police shook their heads and smirked: both kids were referred to the Juvenile Fire Starter Program.

"PLAY THAT FUNKY MUSIC"

I earlier talked about Bobby Flintroy aka, "Cookie Monster": a big man with a big heart. Good thing he has a great sense of humor as well. Occasionally he would bring his saxophone in to practice between calls. He wasn't bad, but for some reason, when you're on the end near the mouthpiece, the sound is more melodious than that at the bell end (where the alleged music comes out).

After several months of listening to him practice, we decided play a practical joke on him. He left his saxophone near his bunk in the dorm and was outside restocking the rescue. While he was outside, I took all the three-hole punches we had in the office to his cubicle and emptied out the paper punches deep into his saxophone where they wouldn't spill out on their own. There were easily hundreds if not thousands of them that went into the instrument. The intent was for us to watch him as he started his practice session and blew the punches into the air.

Of course, the calls started to come in and there was no chance for him to practice. We completely forgot about it until a couple of shifts later when he came to work with this huge grin on his face. We asked what was so funny and he replied that he had gone to his church the previous Saturday and pulled out his saxophone to play for the congregation. When he took a deep breath and started to blow, paper punches flew out of his sax like confetti at a parade. He said everyone was quiet for about five seconds and then the church erupted in laughter. As soon as he realized what had happened, he began to laugh along with them and explained to the congregation that his brother firefighters had played a prank on him. No harm, no foul.

"FREIGHTER RESCUE"

The southeast end of our territory bordered along the Miami River. Many of the freighters carry used bicycles, appliances, old mattresses, drugs in, and cash out to islands like Haiti and the Dominican Republic, and Central America. Some were legitimate, but almost all were old freighters, covered with grease and multiple hull patches holding the ship together. A call came in for a crewmember with a back injury on board one of the freighters docked on the river. Rescue 2 and Squrt 2 responded, and we had to weave our way between hand trucks, containers, hoppers and conveyors to get as close to the ship as possible. We couldn't get any closer than 50 feet due to multiple containers blocking our access. On board, we were guided to the patient who had fallen about 15 feet to the mezzanine floor. He was conscious and alert, but unable to walk. Due to the distance to the Squrt, the only way to get him out was over the edge using a high angle rope rescue. At the time, there were two concurrent TRT calls going on in the County, and the next nearest TRT was over 40 minutes away. Lieutenant Mike Warner, one of the most capable and intelligent fire officers I had the privilege to work with, decided that the best course of action was to immobilize the patient on a backboard and hoist him out hand over hand in a Stokes basket, a metal frame litter used to secure patients for transport in precarious situations like this.

The general rule of thumb when working near an edge of a structure or natural formation is to be tethered to an anchor point. As the area of the ship where we working did not have anything to tie to, we became human anchor points or BFRs (big f%#$ing rocks). In lieu of tying off to a fixed object, four of us doubled up on the rope to hoist him over the edge. Two others guided the Stokes, and the seventh man was on the tagline, guiding the basket as it went up the 25 feet to the main deck. It took us a little over 10 minutes to pull him up and over the edge safely, but over an hour just to get the grease off.

"BLOOD AND SAUSAGE"

For all intents and purposes, the phrase "we're on a 10 (out of service) for decontamination", didn't exist prior to the 1990s. If you worked a trauma call that resulted in a significant amount of blood or other bodily fluids on you, your uniform, or in the truck, you would simply wash it off as quickly and thoroughly as possible to be ready for the next alarm. When all you hear from the communications dispatch center is "Rescue 2 or 7, can you clear? We have calls holding in your territory;" you do what you can to help.

We had latex exam gloves, access to safety glasses and dust masks but that was about it. The best protection was bunker gear but that wasn't always practical. You couldn't walk into someone's home on a gastrointestinal bleed fully bunkered out, or worse, try to work in close quarters on a multi-trauma shooting or stabbing.

Wearing dark blue jumpsuits didn't help. Although the blood couldn't be seen at first glance, you knew the fabric was saturated. You could feel the stickiness penetrating through and making contact with your skin but ignored it and went right back to work.

Years later the crews were issued plastic protective sleeves but the first ones that came out were ridiculously hot and ballooned out at the forearms making us look like flamenco dancers. They would slide down our arms, exposing the skin. The department tried protective disposable coveralls but when they first came out, the one size fits all method was great only if you were 5' 9" and 180 lbs. or smaller. For the rest of us, it was like trying on clothing that was four sizes too small.

Following one shooting with multiple patients, we were soaked with blood, almost from our necks down into our shoes. So much for the use of personal protective equipment (PPE). We were literally slipping in the blood that was on the floor. When we were done with the call, we rinsed off what we could see with saline, cleared, and rushed back to Station 2. This is where the brotherhood of the fire service comes into play. The Squrt crew told us to jump in the shower and they would finish cleaning the truck and run our calls.

We first took a shower with our jumpsuits on, blood running off us like a Grade "B" horror movie at a drive-in. When we washed out almost all the blood we could see, we stripped, and wrung out our clothes to squeeze the last drops out before throwing them in the wash. We stripped, then showered a second time, scrubbing as hard as we could with soap and washcloths trying to get the red tint out of our skin, watching more blood running down the communal drain.

Hal Sears was the first to clean up and changed places with one of the Squrt crew who was in and out running calls on the rescue. Once they changed out, they ran three or four calls back-to-back. While they were still out, we finished cleaning up and jumped on the Squrt for a possible shooting.

When we arrived, it turned out to be an ambush to rob a Domino's Pizza deliveryman. What the bad guys didn't know was that the Domino's employee had a passenger riding with him who was armed. It seems that this wasn't the first time they'd been robbed on a call, but this time they came prepared. Remember, this was before cell phones were prevalent and there was no caller ID. When the robbery went down, the passenger opened fire, but missed the crooks. The bad guys returned fire, grazed the passenger on the arm, and made a run for it. We cleaned and dressed his wound and got ready to clear the scene.

Since the call was bogus, we asked what they were going to do with the pizzas. The driver said they couldn't bring them back to the store and would probably just toss them in the garbage. Seeing that we hadn't eaten all day, we offered to take all three off their hands. They refused our offer to pay for them saying they appreciated our quick response and taking care of them.

It turned out that all three pizzas were sausage but we were starving and didn't care if they were cardboard. We brought them back to the station and ate them like it was a condemned man's last meal: it almost was. We thought that Hal and the other guys on the rescue grabbed something to eat while they were out but we were severely mistaken. When they got back to the station, Hal looked at the empty pizza boxes and almost hulked out. This was a guy who I saw curl a 100-lb. dumbbell five times without breaking a sweat. To placate the Hulk and bring back Dr. Bruce Banner, we quickly ordered a couple more pizzas and picked them up for the crew. It was the first time I ever saw him mad and hopefully the last.

"SAY AGAIN?"

For each patient that we assess, we were required by law to fill out a Florida Emergency Medical Services record, also called a run report. Run reports at that time were printed sequentially, although in reality it didn't matter which report was used, because they all had preprinted identifying numbers on them.

We responded to a vehicular accident with two cars, minor in nature, no serious injuries noted. In this particular case, a set of identical twins were in one of the vehicles, both with similar injuries; minor lacerations to the right forearms. Stranger still, they both had the same first name, and middle initial.

I tried to act casual when I asked the adults why they were both named Demetrius and they looked at me like it was the most normal thing in the world. The father said he liked the name, and since George Foreman named his five sons George Jr., George III, George IV, George V, and George VI, he thought he'd do the same with his. Their middle names were Theodore and Tyrone, which made it even more difficult to document since the run reports only had space for First, Last, and Middle Initials in the section for names.

As expected, the reports went in for processing and were kicked back because the auditors assumed I had written two reports on the same patient. I knew this would happen and could have been avoided by explaining the situation in each narrative, but it was too good not to let it go through.

"PEDESTRIAN VS. PATROL CAR"

As I stated earlier, 22nd Avenue was one of the major thorough-fares in northwest central Miami-Dade County. Some areas of this road were lined with public housing, small Mom and Pop businesses, and houses of worship too many to count. Due to the large number of intersecting roads, it was also the street of choice when attempting to elude police after being involved in criminal activity.

Almost a dead-center impact.

As in any city or neighborhood, most pedestrians do not use cross-walks when crossing a street, as they don't want to take those extra steps to the intersection or wait for the light to change. One particular evening around dusk, an MDPD officer was in route to a call on 22nd

Avenue at a high rate of speed but he apparently had not turned his emergency lights on. As he passed an apartment building, a pedestrian stepped out in front of him. The results were catastrophic, throwing the victim into the air and landing some 30 feet away. When we arrived, we packaged the patient and transported him to the trauma center. The resulting injuries were consistent with what is known as Waddell's Triad: a combination of a femur or long leg bone fracture or fractures, intra-abdominal or intra-thoracic injuries, which are traumatic injuries to internal organs and the protecting skeletal system, and thirdly, injuries to the head. These occur as the initial impact of a vehicle (roughly two-tons in this case) traveling at a high rate of speed comes in contact first with the victim's legs, resulting in the femur fractures. The impact causes the victim to be violently thrown (bent forward) onto the hood of the vehicle, resulting in abdominal or injuries, and finally, the force of the impact throws the victim into, or through the windshield.

A crowd started to form, and several people who weren't even on the scene when the accident occurred, starting murmuring about it being the cop's fault. As time went on, there were more people ready to blame the cop, and to prevent a riot from breaking out, the officer was escorted out of the area for his safety. Eventually, cooler heads prevailed but we never found out if the victim survived.

"THE FUGITIVE"

Early one morning before the official start of our shift, a call for a possible rape came in at around 06:40 hours. My entire crew was already in quarters so we took the call. When we arrived at the scene, there were no police in sight, but there was a lot of commotion coming from a panel van. We decided to investigate and inched closer on foot. We could hear muffled voices coming from inside the van, one definitely being a woman in distress. She was yelling for help, and as we got next to the vehicle, we could make out two blurry, moving shapes through the dirty window. I still couldn't hear any sirens, so I knew we were pretty much on our own at that point.

We flung the doors open and grabbed the attacker by his hair. I yanked him out of the van, naked as a jaybird, and threw him onto the street bouncing on the hard asphalt. Robert Gaitan, one of my partners and I jumped on him and secured him with a pair of flex cuffs that we had obtained from one of the local police units, and my other crewmember quickly checked the woman for injuries. She said she wasn't raped and didn't have any complaints, but the paramedic saw that she only had one arm. Within minutes, several police cruisers showed up, and some of the officers on the scene that we knew fairly well started to laugh when they saw what we had done.

We found out later that she was a prostitute and the situation resulted from a financial dispute with the customer. Of course, we never heard the end of it. At the time, however, we thought differently and were willing to put ourselves at risk to prevent a possible rape.

"CRACK KILLS"

A call came in for a duplex fire. While in route, dispatch advised that the fire was out, but to continue to respond for investigative purposes. When we arrived, a neighbor had two small children with her that had been inside the house during the fire. I assigned a second crew to check the kids for possible injuries or smoke inhalation, went inside with my personnel, and found the origin of the fire: the dead mother of the two children. Evidently, she was "speedballing", or combining heroin and cocaine, a popular habit designed to level out the extreme highs and lows associated with those drugs. Unfortunately, it looked as if she had splashed rubbing alcohol on herself to cool off from the extreme heat and humidity, a common practice and fallacy in the South Florida area. When she lit her pipe to smoke her drugs, the alcohol ignited, spreading to her head and torso. She ran from the living room with her upper body on fire, and thankfully headed toward the bedroom away from the children. Before the alcohol burned away and the fire self-extinguished, she had burned to death. The children were turned over to the Department of Children and Families until family members could be found to pick them up.

"WHAT WAS YOUR NAME AGAIN?"

We were dispatched on a call for a minor vehicle accident and to check for any injuries. When we arrived, my crew did their thing; vital signs, checking for seatbelt, neck pain, etc., while I started the reports. As we normally do, if everyone appears to be uninjured, we'll start with the kids first as a matter of course. I leaned in the passenger window and asked the male passenger who was holding a toddler if he was the father. He said that he was and gave me his name and the name of the child. When I asked if the driver was the mother, he said she was. I then asked him what her name was; he leaned over to her and said, "What's your name again?" Why was I not surprised?

"KENNEL CLUB COLLAPSE"

We were backing into the bay at Station 7 when we heard a call for a possible collapse at the Biscayne Kennel Club, a nine-story, greyhound racetrack grandstand two territories away. Since we were still in the truck, we flipped on the lights and sirens and headed northeast, getting a good jump on other responding units.

When calls were dispatched in the 80s and 90s, the call type and address would be announced on the radio; then the tones at each station would be set off, one by one, with the closest responding unit first. The address was then repeated after the first alarm was completed. As we had almost a minute head start on the other units even before the address was re-announced, we knew we would be one of the first units in.

We arrived seconds after Rescue 30. They were the first due unit who had just established command at the entrance to the racetrack which on first glance, appeared undamaged. Command was set up on what is we now refer to as the Alpha side, or front or address side of the structure, which happened to be on the north side. As there was no visible damage, I directed my crew to drive immediately to the rear of the structure before we were given an assignment. As we made our way around the grandstands, we could now see that the rear of the structure had collapsed into an immense rubble pile of concrete and steel, crushing a pickup truck and a small portable shed.

We quickly found one of the workers who was unhurt and asked where he had run from in order to get a better idea as to where to start the search for possible survivors. He told us that there were several people working on the southwest corner of the partially demolished building when it fell. I advised Command that we were initiating a fast attack to affect a rescue and went to work.

Tons of metal and concrete over our heads.

After searching in and around the area the worker pointed to, we saw three fingers poking out of the rubble. We frantically dug the victim out and found a second partially buried nearby. About 30 minutes after we first arrived, we finally had the second victim out and in route to the trauma center.

During the entire operation, we had nine stories of partially collapsed grandstands and clubhouse hanging over our heads, precariously supported by a mass of metal and concrete. As time went on, we realized we were screaming at each other just to be heard and unable to hear or transmit over our portable hand-held radios. This was due to multiple news helicopters hovering overhead at a few hundred feet, trying to get the best shot possible. Remember, this was years before the super telephoto lenses were in use. Not only was the noise of the helicopters interfering with our transmissions, there was considerable danger from vibrations potentially causing a secondary collapse or loose material dislodging, and either striking or burying us. After they were directed to move back 1,000 feet, we could communicate with each other and Operations. After two-plus hours of digging for other possible survivors, we found two deceased victims, fatally crushed just a few feet from escaping.

I'm in the center in the blue jumpsuit.

Over 30 units and 100 personnel responded to this call, including Florida Task Force 1, one of the two local Urban Search & Rescue teams. This call made the national news and Jeff Strickland, the Captain in charge of Technical Rescue at the time and I were interviewed on Dateline's, "Survivor Series." After an extensive investigation, it was discovered that during demolition, workers inadvertently cut through supporting columns causing the entire structure to collapse.

"INSUBORDINATION"

In most departments, personnel who were equally qualified and had the same rank could trade workdays, as long as it did not exceed that department's specific policy regarding mutual exchange or swap time. MDFR was no different. One of the Lieutenants working at Rescue 26 asked me to cover for him for the first 12 hours on a "C" shift. As I was coming straight from home, I arrived at the firehouse about 06:40 hours. The off-going officer asked if I minded if he left a little early to take his kids to school and of course, I said, no problem. I put my gear on the truck and not two minutes later, the klaxon went off for a chest pain.

The first firefighter/paramedic came out of the dorm less than 30 seconds later, and I asked him where his partner was. He said he thought he was right behind him. A few more seconds went by, but no firefighter. I jumped out of the truck, ran to the entrance of the dorm and yelled, "Let's go, we've got a chest pain." The answer from the bunk was "I'm coming, I'm coming." I ran back to the truck and waited.

In retrospect, I should have left him behind and gone on the call with only the other medic, but I kept thinking, just a few more seconds and he will be here. I reluctantly (and stupidly) continued to wait 30 seconds or so at a time, expecting him at any moment. At almost the six-minute mark, he came strolling out, in absolutely no hurry. I ordered him to get in the truck immediately, but as he was getting in, he felt compelled to come back with, "you need to say good morning first." I was ready to kill him but I directed him not to leave the station before we discussed what occurred.

Luckily, the chest pain turned out to be nothing; we cleared the call about 15 minutes later and returned to the station just after the 07:00 shift change. I did not speak to him in route, as the other firefighter was onboard and it would have been both unprofessional and an uncomfortable situation in the confines of a rescue apparatus. I dropped the report off in the office and asked the other Lieutenant who was also Black to sit in while I counseled the firefighter.

Not surprisingly, he was almost in his car when we looked to the rear parking lot. I ordered him to turn around and go back to the office. He threw his bag down and stalked angrily back to the station. Once there, I directed him to sit down on the opposite side of my desk across from me: he ignored the directive and began pacing back and forth. I advised him that this meeting would be an informal counseling and would not lead to discipline if he understood the magnitude of what had transpired. At that point, I expected him to show some compunction and be apologetic for his actions. Instead, he leaned across my desk and started screaming, "I know about you! I know who you are!"

I sat there unmoving, waiting to see what he would do next. It is interesting how your mind reacts in certain situations. In a matter of seconds, it seemed like I considered multiple response scenarios if he attempted to hit me. I was not overly concerned as I was much bigger than he was, but there was always concern for the possibility of his using something as a weapon to even the odds. It never came to that.

The other Lieutenant quickly stepped in, yelled for him to sit down and shut up, and that he was insubordinate. The firefighter slowly backed off, continued to mumble under his breath and started to leave. The Lieutenant began to stop him but I waved him off to let him go.

At that point, we had no option but to continue with disciplinary actions. I wrote a report on what occurred; the other Lieutenant wrote his memo, and I forwarded it up the chain of command to the appropriate Battalion Chief. In all my years of being a supervisor, this was the first time I had to mete out discipline to someone under my command.

In the early 1990s, a significant amount of departmental documentation including many personnel records were still stored as hard copies. The migration to computer-based records did not become commonplace in our department until the early 2000s. Official records were on file at Headquarters and the Battalion Chiefs kept a second, less extensive file at the battalion where the personnel were assigned. These files would be sent to other battalions when the personnel were reassigned. At times, files were incomplete, resulting in inconsistent record keeping, and some outright failures to follow up on a few individuals who required coaching, counseling, behavior modification, or if necessary, discipline.

In order to obtain access to the official files, the policy required that we go to the Personnel Department in the Human Resources Division, indicate that we were the individual's primary supervisor, or provide a valid reason for reviewing the files. The distance alone stopped some officers from getting involved to begin with, as they did not want to put in the extra hours. Miami-Dade County is almost 60 linear miles from end to end and the traffic is some of the worst in the country. Others chose not to pursue the process, as there was a deep-rooted perception that it would go nowhere and was a waste of time.

When I signed in at the Personnel Department, they offered me a desk and brought his files. As I began to look through page after page, I could not believe the number of policy violations and recent questionably unlawful actions that this individual had in his file. Less than three weeks earlier, another officer wrote him up for not responding in a timely manner and the paperwork had yet to be processed. There was an accusation of slapping a patient in the back of a different Rescue but there were no witnesses. He supposedly pulled a gun in a traffic dispute, and charges were pending.

No progressive discipline, never relieved of duty, nothing. Somehow, through a lack of shift-to-shift continuity and the ability to move from firehouse to firehouse and away from ongoing scrutiny, he had fallen through the cracks. My report was processed and forwarded up the chain of command. Not surprisingly, a few months later he tested positive for cocaine during a physical and was terminated.

What did he mean by "I know about you?" A few days after the 9/11 World Trade Center attack, the County Manager and the Fire Chief ordered all fire stations and apparatus to fly the American flag in honor of the firefighters and police officers killed in the terrorist attacks. While we working at the World Trade Center, several of us were approached by firefighters from FDNY who were visibly angry and demanded to know, "What the Hell is wrong with your department?" I had no idea what they were talking about until they showed us a newspaper article identifying three Miami-Dade firefighters who allegedly refused to ride on a truck with an American flag flying from it. At first, I was stunned, then enraged. I told them that if the story were true, then they should fire the scumbags. Apparently, a reporter overheard my comments and printed them in a local tabloid. The comments got back to the department, and as usual, blown out of proportion and in this case made into a racial issue. I stand by those comments to this day: they were scumbags.

"COLD AS ICE"

Normally, firefighters assigned to a station had a locker for the duration of that assignment. The purpose of that locker was to stow your uniforms and personal belongings. Bunker gear was stored separately in outside lockers to allow for off-gassing of fire-related products that were accumulated during the shift. Some didn't get it and continued to leave their gear out in the communal areas. To assist them in remembering, we would try, shall we say, productive means of coercion.

The first one who learned not to leave his uniforms hanging in the day room was a rookie. He immediately had a second strike against him just for being on probation. He left his nicely pressed button-down gray work shirt hanging in the day room with his badge and nametag still attached. As it was nearing St. Patrick's Day, we decided the best course of action was to show our Irish pride and color his silver badge Shamrock green (or as close to it as possible). We used a green felt marker, which worked quite nicely, and could be cleaned with a little elbow grease.

When he returned the following shift, we heard the probie had a lot to say about our destroying County property and blabbering about making a complaint. When his Battalion Chief heard what happened, he reamed him for leaving his gear behind and making threats against veteran firefighters who took care of their County-assigned property. He shut up and never left his gear out again.

We started to get more creative with others who left their uniforms out. We stuffed shirts into five-pound coffee cans with the tip of the badge sticking out and would freeze it, letting the victim know where to find it. Another one of our firefighters left his out on a hangar, neatly pressed. We decided to lay it in a baking pan filled with cold water and the hangar sticking out. We laid it down carefully in a freezer and let nature do its work. After two days, it was encased in a frozen block of translucent ice, like a perfectly preserved fossil out of the Pleistocene period. An hour before he reported for duty, we hung it in the engine bay where it continually dripped until he could chip off the remaining ice. He appreciated the humor and did say that after the initial shock of putting the shirt on, it actually felt pretty good. Eventually, word got around, and gear was stowed in its proper places, at least in our battalion.

"TRENCH WARFARE"

Every neighborhood has that one eccentric: the loner. Quiet, keeps to himself, and is typically unknown to everyone else until something happens, and that something is usually not good. We've seen too many times where this goes south, resulting in someone saying, "I always knew something wasn't right, but it wasn't my business" or, "I didn't want to get involved." This could have easily been one of those situations had it not turned out the way it did.

The call came in for a man down: the type of call we received a dozen times every week. When we arrived, the front yard of this single-family home looked like it had been attacked by giant moles. The yard had been almost completely dug up with piles of dirt everywhere. Upon closer inspection, we found dozens of trenches almost three feet deep and two feet wide traversing the entire front and back yards.

We heard a muffled voice coming from one of the trenches and had to search through the maze until we found the owner of the house, lying on his side, partially covered with dirt. He could move but he couldn't get up by himself. His speech was slurred and he couldn't move his left side. He appeared to have been digging in the trench and had a stroke almost two days before. He repeatedly tried to call for help but without success. He was exhausted and dehydrated but still alive. Once we secured him on a backboard, we lifted him out, gave him oxygen and started an IV to hydrate him. When we got him to the hospital, we used the outside decontamination shower to wash the dirt off him and to look for additional possible injuries.

When the police arrived at the hospital, they advised that he was a Vietnam veteran who had bipolar disorder, or what was more commonly known at the time as manic-depression. They also found hundreds of weapons in his home, ranging from shotguns, a dozen M16 rifles and M1 carbines, various handguns, and tens of thousands of rounds of ammunition. Once the weapons were discovered, there were concern over his having flashbacks and thinking he was back in Vietnam. There was no telling what his ultimate plans were had he not suffered a stroke.

"CLIPBOARD? WHAT CLIPBOARD?"

One of the firefighters we knew who finally promoted to Lieutenant decided to bid Station 7, primarily because of the people who worked there. He was a great guy, but more than a little cynical. The third medic on the truck that day was a rookie who was probably on the job for no more than two to three weeks.

We responded to a call for a possible stroke. When we arrived at the house, I knocked on the door and an elderly woman answered. We asked what the problem was, and she replied that her husband was not acting right. She invited us in and when we entered, we noticed a man in his late 70s or early 80s, probably no more than 120 lbs. He showed obvious signs of an old stroke as he had minimal movement in his right arm and was dragging his right leg. We asked the wife what was different today, and she answered, "nothing, this is how he always is." This is typical of many calls received by Fire Rescue and Police; the call comes in as a stroke and upon arrival, we find it's actually a shooting. We get the call for a heart attack, and it's someone who's been sick with a cold for three weeks. On the other hand, we get a call from someone with a stomach ache, and it turns out to be a massive heart attack.

Once again, we asked her, but what is the problem today and why did you call 911? While trying to obtain his history from his wife and reviewing a long list of his current medications, the old man began circling around the Lieutenant like a lion around his prey. The Lieutenant told the patient very nicely, "come on, sit down next to your wife and let us take a look at you." The patient sat quietly for a few seconds and decided to get up. The Lieutenant sat him down again, and again he got up.

Out of the blue, he clamped down on the Lieutenant's arm, mouth wide open in attack mode. However, as his teeth were in a glass in the bathroom, he was more or less trying to gum the Lieutenant to death. At the time, however, the Lieutenant didn't know the man was toothless and jumped back in a purely defensive maneuver. When the old man continued his somewhat feeble assault, the Lieutenant used his clipboard as a shield and thumped him lightly in the head, sending him falling backward into a bookcase. The rookie and I grabbed the man before he fell and sat him down in the chair.

His wife put a bowl of cereal in front of him and he started eating as if nothing ever happened. I looked at the rookie, whose eyes were as big as saucers thinking, OMG, I'm going to lose my job! The patient and his wife acted as if nothing out of the ordinary had taken place. We finished our exam and his wife said she would call his doctor for a follow up appointment. Three weeks later, we returned on another non-emergency call on the same man, but neither he nor his wife recognized us or mentioned the previous visit.

"IS THAT A VENTRILOQUIST IN YOUR PANTS?"

The Lieutenant on Squrt 2 told me that he had returned from a call that topped anything he had ever seen. He said that his last call was an obstetrical, or pregnancy call. When he and his crew arrived, a young woman in her 20's told him that she needed to go to the hospital because she was going to have a baby. She didn't appear to be pregnant or in any distress, so he continued to ask her for information to determine his course of action.

As he continued, he heard crying coming from the crotch of her pants. It turned out that she had delivered the baby just before the crew arrived but didn't bother to take off her pants or attempt to get the newborn out. Needless to say, they cut her pants off, began providing support measures, and called for a Rescue for transport. Talk about an easy delivery: the mother had no idea that she had given birth. The Lieutenant was laughing so hard when he told the story I thought he was going to pee all over himself.

"NEVER LEAVE A FRIEND BEHIND"

We found a guy lying next to a payphone (yeah, hundreds of years ago before cell phones were commonplace) who was obviously dead. His buddy had dragged him about two blocks to the phone in order to call 911 after the victim had overdosed on heroin. It took his Good Samaritan friend about 30 to 40 minutes to drag him to the payphone but it only took us about 30 seconds to pronounce him, and another two minutes to get the police on-scene.

What's amazing is that less than three hours after the evening rush hour, he dragged his friend near one of the busier roads in the vicinity, and no one thought twice about calling the police for what most would normally consider a rather unusual occurrence. As far as we know, the friend was never charged with anything except chronic stupidity.

"THERE'S NO CASTE SYSTEM IN THIS COUNTRY!"

South Florida is home to many of the wealthiest people in the country, and some of the poorest as well. By and large, they move in distinctly separate circles, but at times there is unavoidable interaction. Most of the time it involves the homeless attempting to wash the windshields of the Bentleys, Mercedes, and other luxury cars for a quarter in downtown Miami.

Two different worlds momentarily colliding.

In this particular incident, unless they were slumlords checking on their decrepit investments in a run-down area, these high-enders were way out of their element. They say a picture is worth a thousand words. In this case, we had an elderly Caucasian male dressed in all white getting out of a white Rolls Royce, next to a destitute Black man wearing multiple layers of clothing and having a urinary catheter sticking out of his clothes. It conjures up a Salvadore Dali-esque image. Nothing more can or needs to be said.

"CORNER OFFICE"

The Firehouse 2 "reception area/lobby" was no more than 300 square feet. It also doubled as the office space for both the Rescue and Aerial officers. This spacious area included a rip and run (dot matrix) printer, the medical equipment supply closet, and the desks that were straight out of the 1950s with updated 1960s swivel chairs. It wasn't the best working environment, and certainly not conducive when dealing with personnel who have work-related or personal issues. If we had to discuss something in a more private setting, we would use the Battalion Chief's office if he was out, or we would have to walk out into one of the bays for privacy.

Attached to the wall above the Rescue officer's desk was a three-slot wooden box. The slots were marked "A", "B", and "C" for each shift's officer to submit their run reports. As the Rescue Captain, my administrative responsibilities included reviewing daily run reports from both crews on the other two shifts. The 60 to 100 reports that I reviewed every third day were at times stacked 30 to 40 high on the desk when the box that was designed to hold them overflowed. This was long before the conversion to a computer-based system, and each report had to be reviewed by hand; line by line, word for word.

Since the immediate area around the Rescue officer's desk was about 50 square feet, I decided to "enclose" it. In feigning that I actually had a modicum of privacy, I marked off the area around my desk with masking tape. To add to the ambiance, I added a door with an exterior swing direction on the floor, similar to what you find on architectural plans. I then put an old doorknob on floor and a handwritten sign on the wall that read, "Please knock". When anyone (except the Chief of course) approached and spoke to me, I ignored them until they pretended to knock. The crews would either tap their foot on the floor or say "knock, knock" to play along. Other crews that were passing through or personnel assigned to the station for the day did a double take when they saw the tape or just shake their head and snicker.

"I READ IT IN A MANAGEMENT BOOK"

When I first joined the department almost 40 years ago, the only formal recognition process for those who went beyond the call of duty was "Firefighter of the Month." This award could be bestowed only to a single individual, as there was no course of action to honor multiple personnel, either while in uniform or on personal time.

Unfortunately, at times it seemed to be more of an obligatory gesture than a true appreciation of service. When the monthly recipient was decided on, the administration distributed an all stations memo to inform the troops which was shared at the morning briefing. A nice gesture, but when you had more than one firefighter whose actions far surpassed normal expectations and only one received recognition, it left something to be desired.

Then, without any input from firefighters in Operations, the award was arbitrarily changed to "Employee of the Month". Now firefighters putting their lives on the line were actually in competition with civilian employees, with some working in an office setting exposed to unspeakable dangers such as a papercut or carpal tunnel syndrome. This went on for a few years with occasional grumbling from the crews in Operations, but no one stepped forward in an attempt to change the process.

Then a firefighter on restricted duty won the award for identifying and developing markers for hydrants that were out of service in a trailer park. During that same month, we had nominated a crew of three firefighters who saved two victims in a house fire. When we complained about the snub, the response was that they selected the individual over the others because there was no mechanism to honor a crew. We could not believe what we had heard, and after speaking to others across the County who experienced similar issues, we knew it was time for a change.

A handful of personnel requested a meeting with the Fire Chief with the intent of creating a top-quality system of honoring the men and women of the department. He approved the formation of a steering committee and the research process was set in motion. They first identified, and then contacted multiple fire and law enforcement departments across the country that had successful programs in place.

In 2001, the Fire Chief retired, leading to an organizational change and the County Manager appointing a new Fire Chief. As typically occurs, the new Chief puts a hold on all pending projects until he or a designee could review them and determine if they met his agenda. The new Deputy Chief now had oversight of the yet to be approved Meritorious Service policy and Board of Merit, which would be comprised of personnel who volunteered their time and efforts to establish a formal recognition process.

One of the other Captains and I requested a meeting with him to try to push the program through. We showed him the years of work already put in to recognize both uniform and civilian personnel, single and multiple units, and members of the public for acts of valor, meritorious service, and personal excellence, and examples of personnel who would have unquestionably received medals of valor had the program been in place.

The Deputy Chief hesitated, questioned us about cost, and seemed to be against moving forward. We realized that since this was a holdover program from the previous administration, we would really have to sell it to him. We pushed the issue, explained that this was a win-win situation, and a tremendous morale builder. We also explained that there was zero cost as we were all donating our time and efforts, and that the new administration could take full credit for implementing the program. We told him we were ready for what we wanted to call Medal Day.

He sat for a few minutes thinking about it and finally answered, "I know that it's good for morale; I read that in a management book". I had to keep the other Captain from jumping out of his chair, doing something he would definitely regret, and possibly ending his career on the spot. Fortunately, nothing was said and the Deputy Chief gave us permission to proceed. We thanked the Chief for his time, exited his office and went to work.

The Board of Merit and the subsequent annual Medal Day ceremony became a reality. As of this writing, Medal Day has been held annually for over two decades honoring thousands of men and women who would have otherwise gone unrecognized. I was elected as Chair of the Board of Merit in 2001 and was honored to serve as Chair for 10 consecutive years, the longest tenure by anyone in the department. In order to ensure continuity and to turn over the reins in a timely manner, I voluntarily stepped aside one year before I retired in 2012. I remained on the Board until my last day with the department.

"LOVE IS BLIND (AND ON DRUGS)"

Battalion 5 was the focal point for several Metrorail stations, the local elevated rapid transit system. As such, we had many "customers" who would hang out at the stations, panhandling or sleeping it off. One Sunday morning we received a call for difficulty breathing at one of the stations. When we arrived, one of the police officers on-scene apologized for calling us. He said they were arresting a crackhead and her boyfriend when she decided that it would be better to go to the hospital than to jail and started to complain that she couldn't breathe. Both of the perpetrators were in their 20's, and with the exception of what crack cocaine does to the human body, in relatively good shape. We took her vital signs (normal, especially her respiratory rate and blood oxygen saturation level) and gave them the ok to be transported by police. When she insisted that she needed to go to the hospital because she couldn't breathe, and then the boyfriend decided he wanted the same, we put a nasal cannula (provides low flow oxygen directly into the nostrils) on her and told him to blow into the other end. Then we put a nasal cannula on him and told her to blow into the other end of his tube. After two or three minutes, both of them realized that transportation to the County hospital was not in their immediate future, and they started feeling better. They were released to the police and we hit the road for the next call.

Breathe deep!

"NOT ALWAYS READY OR PROUD TO SERVE"

As I expressed earlier, the fire service is not for everyone. Some look at firefighting for the benefits and hours but are not willing to meet the Miami-Dade Fire Rescue Mission Statement they swore to uphold. That Mission Statement is "Always Ready, Proud to Serve: We protect people, property and the environment by providing responsive professional and humanitarian fire rescue services essential to public health, safety and well-being". Unfortunately, that was not always true.

More than two dozen officers from the Miami-Dade County Department of Corrections made the choice to switch from a detention-based law enforcement organization to that of saving lives and property. Many were and are outstanding, but one in particular left something to be desired.

In the late 90's, a call came in for a house fire in Station 2's territory. Squrt 2 was on another call and Engine 7 was dispatched as the first due suppression unit. I was on Rescue 2 riding heavy (one extra-unassigned firefighter) and we were just clearing from another call nearby. It was one of those days when all the dispatchers were slammed with call after call and all the frequencies, especially Central, was filled with units being dispatched or asked to clear for another call. Rescue 2 arrived just ahead of Engine 7, but I couldn't even get on the air to give an arrival.

We were on the south side of the structure and all four of us were headed to the front of the house that had flames blowing out at least three windows. Not a big deal since it was a small, approximately 1,800 square foot house. Engine 7 arrived on the west side and since they could see us rounding the corner but hadn't yet heard us, stated code and conditions and made it a Code 2 for units on the scene. A Code 1 was a first alarm (full assignment, working fire), a Code 2 was handled by a specific unit or units, and a Code 3 was an investigation being done by the first arriving unit.

When the Captain (Gary Pilger again) first saw us, he thought we were another suppression unit and Rescue 2 was coming right behind. I told him that it's just us, and we're on our own. As most of us worked together for years, we would occasionally mix and match crews, depending on who was working that shift. One of my crewmembers and a rookie from Engine 7 who happened to be one of those former corrections officers who had no business wearing the uniform, stayed with me in order to make entry through the front exterior door and to give the rookie some experience with forcible entry. Engine 7, along with one of my partners, Robert Gaitan, went in from the west side of the house and knocked down the fire at that end of the structure. Gaitan is another good friend who I would trust with my life and my family, anytime, anywhere.

We used a halligan (single piece, 30", nine-lb. forged steel rod with a wedge-shaped fork at one end and an adz at the other end), a flat-head axe and a 10-lb. sledge to pry open the door. As we forced the door open, heavy smoke and heat vented through the doorway. The rookie was crouching with the nozzle in hand, and I was just behind him leaning over his shoulder with my hands on my knees, taking considerably more heat from the rollover. He started to panic, yelling through his mask that the roof was collapsing. I tried to keep him calm and told him, "No it's only pieces of the ceiling coming down. Let's get inside and knock it down now." When he started screaming louder that it was too hot, I told him again, "let's go, now!" He hesitated and then completely froze. I grabbed the hose line, cursing loudly enough to probably be heard at the other end of the house. My other crewmember and I quickly moved past him, hitting the main body of fire. Once we extinguished the fire along with Engine 7's crew and started overhaul (checking for fire extension and hot spots to prevent a rekindle), we doffed our gear to cool off. The rook went to Captain Pilger to complain about what I had done, and that my actions resulted in getting him burned. When asked to explain what he meant, the rookie showed him mild second-degree burns on his neck and his ears. Gary told him that he had no problem taking the complaint up the chain of command to the Battalion Chief, but did he really want to do that since it sounded as if he had forgotten to put on his protective Nomex hood? He backed off and shut his mouth. Somehow, he passed probation but as time went on, this individual continued to have problems, both on scenes and interacting with brother and sister firefighters.

As the saying goes, what goes around comes around. Six years later, this same individual was arrested after impersonating a police officer, abducting a 20-year-old mentally challenged man and sexually assaulting him. He's back in the Corrections system, only now he's looking out from behind bars where he belongs.

"BROTHERLY LOVE"

It's a normal thing for siblings to argue. Mostly it's a civilized disagreement, at times escalating to the raising of voices or perhaps being given the silent treatment. Now and then, it even comes to fisticuffs. Rarely does it involve weapons, especially when one of the them feels compelled to leave the scene and return 45 minutes later with a 30-30 rifle and shoot his brother in the knee. The damage done by an exploding cartridge is amazing. The entrance wound is significant but the exit wound is an opening the size of a child's fist, ripping through bone, cartilage and tendons. What's also amazing is the total lack of remorse the shooter showed for the victim, his own brother.

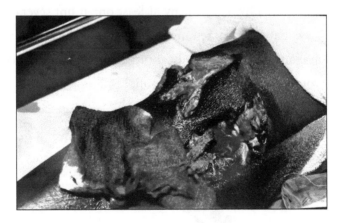

In one side, out the other.

"DRIVE BY SHOOTING"

Just another shooting: this time they left something behind. A still running car, front seats stained with blood, and a partially loaded and recently fired AR-15 on the front seat. The target was someone in the Scott-Carver projects who happened to have enough weaponry to fight back, causing considerable damage of their own. In this particular incident, there were over 70 bullet holes in the buildings and shell casings on both the street and alleyway behind the projects. Remarkably, no one in the street or any of the apartments, usually filled with dozens of people ranging from toddlers to senior citizens, was injured. Whomever the shooter (or shooters) were in the car left behind, they were obviously hit by at least one if not several bullets. I have to say, it always amazed me that these morons would show up at a hospital and think that medical professionals couldn't recognize a bullet wound or wouldn't call the police.

More of these started to show up years later.

"WE'RE ON OUR OWN"

The Miami-Dade School system was the fourth largest school district in the country and to support that system, several maintenance facilities were strategically located across the County. A fuel tanker was offloading fuel at one of those facilities located in the south end of Station 2's territory when a fire broke out. It quickly accelerated, jumping to a nearby vehicle and a large warehouse. Just as Squrt and Rescue 2 arrived, the tanker ruptured, creating a huge fireball. The heat from the fire was unbelievable; we could feel it as soon as we got out of the truck and we were at least 100 feet from the main body of fire. I had a Kodak Instamatic camera with me and took two quick pictures as I came out of the back of the rescue. I threw the camera back into the truck and ran to the Squrt and helped pull the 200-foot jump line with one of the firefighters from Squrt 2.

Starting to stretch hose.

Two others grabbed the other jump line and all of us got as close to the tanker as possible and lay flat on the ground to keep from getting cooked. The rest of the crews worked together to set up an elevated master stream and checked for victims. Normally, HazMat and one or more of the foam trucks from Miami International Airport would respond, but they were on two other major incidents going on simultaneously. We had a minimal amount of foam and went through it in no time. It seemed like we were there for hours before the next unit arrived, but it was actually no more than 10 minutes. By the time we got the fire under control, the tanker, which was on a slight incline, had spilled hundreds of gallons of burning fuel that caused a running fuel fire, incinerating two buildings and seven vehicles in a parking lot.

Timing is everything.

Several weeks later, I brought the film in to be developed. When the pictures came back, the second photo at the fire scene showed

Lt. Mike Warner in the frame with the fireball in the background. A second earlier, his helmet would have blocked the fireball, and any later, he would have been out of the frame entirely: pure luck.

"HEADACHE REMOVER"

One particular gentlemen who was a frequent flyer (one who utilizes Fire Rescue services on a regular basis) called with a headache for eight (yes, eight) years. After examining him and taking his vital signs, we realized that he was just looking for a ride downtown. Many of our frequent flyers used to call 911 and complain of some sort of ailment that would require transportation to Jackson Memorial Hospital, enabling them to go about their business downtown without the cost of a taxi ride. Since we couldn't technically refuse at least ambulance transportation, they would be sent to the hospital. Once they'd arrive, they would refuse treatment and take off, and some would literally walk in the ER entrance and right out another door. The big question was how they always seemed to be able to get back to call us again and again.

We cured our friend with the headache by taking a bag-valve-mask, aka, ambu-bag (used to provide oxygen) and rearranging the straps so they wrapped around his head; when he blew into an attached tube, the bag that was strapped to the top put pressure on his head, relieving him of the headache. He was happy, we were happy and he didn't have to go to the hospital.

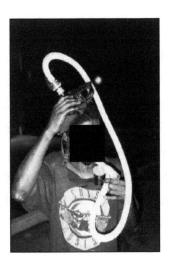

That feels much better!

"MOTHER AND CHILD LOST"

Unfortunately, bad things sometimes happen to good people. A woman was driving an SUV westbound on a surface street that merged into an expressway and at the same time, another SUV was headed southbound on the intersecting avenue. Tragically, both vehicles entered the intersection at the same time, resulting in both SUVs rolling over and landing on their sides. Rescues 7 and 26, Engine 7, and Aerial 26 arrived at approximately the same time. We made contact with the woman in the first SUV but could barely reach her arm and upper body. Both legs were crushed and pinned under the dashboard and frame that had been pushed back into the passenger compartment onto her. She was pulseless, in cardiac arrest, and worse, it turned out she was eight months pregnant. The SUV was tilted precariously on the rear quarter panel and a section of the front and ready to fall over onto its roof. One of our firefighters climbed on top of the SUV in order to climb in to start CPR, and four of us physically held the SUV upright until we could support it with cribbing. Meanwhile, other crews were attending to the occupants of the other vehicle who were also badly injured, although not as critical. Almost five minutes into the extrication, we realized that it would take us 20-30 minutes to get her out due to the damage to the vehicle and the way she was pinned. Both she and the baby would die if extraordinary measures were not taken.

An unfortunate situation.

Normally, trauma surgeons would be flown in from JMH if the patient was viable, but in this case, we were fighting a losing battle. We knew that the mother would not make it and requested the approval to perform an emergency caesarian section. This was not in our protocols and had never been done in a pre-hospital setting that we knew of but we had nothing to lose by asking and hoping the trauma center would allow it and walk us through the procedure.

Unfortunately, after several minutes of nerve-wracking discussion at their end, they denied our request and chose not to go through with it. By the time we extricated the mother and got her to the hospital, she was pronounced dead as was her fetus.

What made this call even more bizarre was that after the police were looking at the paperwork, they compared them and found that both vehicles were identical white Ford Explorers rented from the same agency on the same day, and both drivers, although unrelated, had the same last name of Rodriguez.

"THE ONE MUSKETEER"

When I was first promoted to Lieutenant, I was given the option of switching from 'A' to 'B' platoon in order to stay at Station 2 or be reassigned to one of the slower stations. To me it was a no-brainer. In order to stay at the firehouse I now considered be my home base, I was definitely willing to switch shifts. The only downside to this was that this was three months before the holidays and 'A' shift would be off on Christmas that year while 'B' shift would have to work. I asked my Battalion Chief Mike Simons, and the 'B' shift Battalion Chief Dave Brooks, if it was possible to make the switch but go back to 'A' shift prior to Christmas as my family had already made plans for the holidays. Both Chiefs said, "no problem, we'll make it happen." One of things I liked about the leadership at Battalion 5 was that if they said they were going to do something; we knew they'd back it up. I never mentioned it again.

Now back to the story. The Lieutenant on Squrt 2 on 'B' shift was a relatively short, heavyset, ass-kicker of a firefighter. You'd look at him and think there was no way he could do the job due to his weight and size but he could run circles around most firefighters, me included. One of the rookies assigned to me on Rescue 2 was a kid who was definitely excited to be in the fire service and talked a mile a minute. After one of our many structure fires, the rookie went in to take a shower. He had taken a clean uniform out of his locker and hung it near the showers but he had left his locker door open. The rookie was a tall thin kid and probably had about a 26-inch waist. We took the uniform hanging by the shower as well as his dirty uniform on the floor, every other uniform and piece of clothing that he had in his locker and hid them all. In their place, we left one of the Lieutenant's uniforms. Unfortunately for the rookie, the Lt.'s waist size was well over 40 inches and he was about four inches shorter than the kid was. When the rookie got out the shower, the only thing we had left him was a pair of his own underwear. He had no choice but to put on the Lieutenant's extra uniform.

This is one for which I wish I had pictures. The shirt hung off him as if it belonged to his father. Even better, he had an extra 14 to 16 inches at the waistline but had no belt and had to hold the pants up with his hands. You could've almost put another kid his size inside the pants with him. On top of that, the pants were about four inches too short and it looked like he was ready for a flood. This was only about midway through the 24-hour shift and we knew we had in the least another dozen or so calls to run.

To make matters worse, one of the other firefighters decided to give him a mustache similar to those worn by the Three Musketeers. One small problem; we didn't know it at the time but he used a permanent marker. Well, it never fails: as soon as he was outfitted, they toned us out for a call. Now on most calls, probationary firefighters are required to take the patient's vital signs, including the blood pressure. I don't remember what the complaint was, but when we got to the house, the rookie kneeled down in front of the patient and began to put a blood pressure cuff around her arm. He had attached clothespins to his pants in order to hold them up which drew her attention. With a puzzled look, the patient's gaze went from his oversized pants to his freshly drawn D'Artagnon-style moustache. He couldn't look her in the eye and kept focused on the task at hand. She looked at me like, "did I miss something?" I simply shrugged my shoulders and said "new guy."

"SANTERIA"

South Florida is a multicultural, multiracial, amalgam of society with residents and visitors from across the world. A large number come from South and Central America and the Caribbean islands, including Cuba and the island that comprises the Dominican Republic and Haiti. Although they come to this country for a better life, this influx of immigrants commonly remains loyal to their individual cultures, religions, and traditions.

Living and working in South Florida, it was inevitable that we as pre-hospital caregivers would eventually respond to calls involving Santeria (Duncan, 2008). Santeria is an Afro-Cuban religion that came to South Florida with the Cuban exile community and had exponential growth after the 1980s Mariel boatlift. It blends African religion with some aspects of Christianity by portraying various African deities with comparisons to Roman Catholic saints. This is known as syncretism, or combining different, often seemingly contradictory beliefs. For the most part, Santeria has been a benign practice in this country with the exception of ritual animal sacrifice, ruled on by the Supreme Court that banning it violated the First Amendment's guarantee of the free exercise of religion.

There were three incidents that I can clearly recall that involved Santeria, although I'm sure there were many more, not only by our particular stations, but across the County. The first time I came in contact with Santeria in the fire service was while fighting a small house fire. A perpetually lit candle inside a small wooden cabinet built as a shrine had over many years slowly dried out the residual moisture in the wood, eventually leading to thermal degradation and causing the cabinet to burst into flames. Shrines are constructed as altars to ancestors; typically found on a white cloth with a white candle, three or more glasses of water (it has to be an odd number), food offerings, flowers, prayers, and cigar smoke. Some shrines are actually set aside in their own room or their own building.

The second was a little more interesting; another house fire, but a little more intense, with heavy smoke emanating from the kitchen after a pot was left unattended on the stove (see South Florida kitchen renovation). As the smoke began to clear, I noticed a small shrine in a corner not far from the front door. On the table were the typical items I previously mentioned, but in addition were three black dolls; two made of cloth, and one of porcelain, all in what appeared to be calico dresses. As Haitian Vodou (Voodoo) is sometimes confused with Santeria and uses dolls like these to house human and spiritual influences of individuals, this may not have been Santeria, but actually a Vodou shrine. The porcelain doll was on the floor near the shrine. There had been a lot of movement in the house with hose lines and personnel, so I assumed the table was bumped, knocking the doll to the floor. I picked it up and put it back with the others. About 10 minutes later, I noticed the same doll on the floor again, but a few feet further away from the shrine and closer to the front door. Once again, I replaced it and continued assisting with clearing the smoke from the house. A few minutes later, I saw the same porcelain doll on the floor about a foot outside the front door. I picked it up and decided that if it really wanted out, it was going with me. I placed it in inside the one and one-half inch inner tube on my helmet alongside the door chocks (wedges) and went outside. A couple of the Cuban-American firefighters saw it, shook their heads and said "not a good idea." When I came out with the it on my helmet, some of the firefighters took a few steps away.

I don't believe in the occult and have a habit of being extremely irreverent toward those beliefs. I also know that many professionals outwardly state they don't believe either but are hesitant to take the next step in dismissing them as hogwash. The doll stayed on my helmet for several years but then one Saturday night I worked overtime at Station 27, one of the slower stations in the County.

After I got to the station, I put my gear on the bay floor waiting for the rescue crew to return from a call. Somehow, the porcelain doll that had been in my helmet band for a few years and had seen multiple calls, worked itself loose and wound up on the bay floor. When the rescue backed in, it rode right over the doll, breaking it into several pieces. No one had been near my gear or touched the helmet. I thought it was strange but wrote it off to coincidence. Since then, I have had ongoing problems with desktop computers, laptops, cellphones and anything tied to technology. Coincidence? Not according to many I worked with of Caribbean descent.

The third incident again involved a house fire, but this was one was a little different. As in many religions, there are individuals who follow extreme ideologies. In this case, we found a large glass jar, probably around ten gallons in the center of a shrine on the back porch. When we first looked at the jar, we weren't sure what we were looking at and had to do a double take. It was filled with thousands of dollars in cash in multiple denominations, including twenties, fifties and hundreds. That in itself was a surprise, but what we saw next was something that could not have been imagined. Inside the liquid-filled jar was a human fetus with the umbilical cord still attached. We immediately notified the police but never found out who was responsible or how they obtained the fetus. The word on the street was that he was a former physician from Cuba who dabbled in Santeria.

"LARGE RESPONSE TEAM PART DEAUX"

As I previously stated, there were more than 40 patients that weighed over 500 lb. in the two adjoining territories. This particular call involved another "plus, plus, plus size" patient; again, in her 20's with absolutely no concept of when to say no to food. On this call, we found the young lady in the back bedroom (why are they always in the back of the house or on the second floor?) lying on the bed unable to move. This one also had difficulty breathing (what a surprise!), but the difference was that there was a five-pound bucket of fried chitterlings next to the bed. Chitterlings, also called chitlins, are pig or hog intestines and are popular in some of the economically deprived communities. Like anything else, fried food in moderation is ok, but when your diet consists of five or more pounds daily.... When we asked her father about the chitlins, he said something to the effect "she can't get out of the bed and keeps getting fatter." One of our guys couldn't hold back and said "Sir, I think you can solve both problems by not bringing the chitlins to her. At least she'll get some exercise by going to the kitchen."

Well, since we were now "certified" as a Large Response Team (remember, Bariatric Transport not only did not exist but wasn't even part of the thought process in the 80's), I jokingly advised dispatch that we had an LRT call. The dispatcher of course had no clue what I was talking about and I had to tell her to disregard the last transmission. However, I knew the other crews from Stations 2 and 7 were monitoring their radios and would respond. When they arrived, we had already developed a plan to extricate her.

Once again, multiple backboards were strapped together, but instead of oxygen tanks, we laid a roof ladder outside her bedroom and put her and the backboards onto the aluminum ladder, allowing us to slide her out to the front door. We then lashed the whole contraption together and put the patient and ladder inside the rescue. The only problem was that we couldn't close the back doors of the truck. Since it was dusk, we attached two large, bulky flashlights to the tip of the ladder hanging outside the truck, stood on the ladder closest to the front of the cab to weight it down and brace it. The engine company follow us to the hospital as we drove at about five mph with our emergency lights on. By the way, this time the hospital was ready for us and had an extra-large hospital bed waiting. We slid the backboards off the ladder onto the bed and once the paperwork was completed, cleared for the next call.

"HURRY, PEDAL FASTER!"

One of the greatest things about working in the firehouse is the camaraderie. For the most part, the individuals working there get along regardless of their ethnicity or race. One can also expect that if you play a practical joke on someone, you can usually assume payback is on the horizon. It may come days, weeks, or months later, but it will come.

One of my partners, Marcos "Ace" Acevedo decided to play one of those jokes on Manny Morales. Unfortunately, Ace had an extremely short memory for this particular prank he pulled on Manny. A few hours later while we had some downtime, Ace went to the exercise room to work out on the stationary bike. When Manny realized where he was, he told us it was payback time and wanted us to create a minor diversion. His intent was to bring a charged (pressurized) hose line into the workout room to provide Ace with an unscheduled shower.

Ace was in the back corner of the room, facing the doorway. I walked in first, a couple of the other guys followed me, and then Manny came in behind us with the hose line. Now, hoses used in firefighting come in several sizes. We had a one-inch diameter booster hose on a reel, a one and three-quarter inch, and a two and one-half inch line. Manny decided the hose of choice for this mission was the one and three-quarter which flowed 95 to 200 gallons per minute. This was the equivalent of a bathtub of water being dumped on you in less than 60 seconds. When Ace looked up and made eye contact with Manny, it didn't quite register as to what was going to happen. When Ace finally looked down at the hose in Manny's hands, he realized he was dead meat. Instead of getting off the bike and running for it, he instinctively started pedaling faster and faster as if he would get away on the stationary bike. It was hilarious to watch, especially when Manny opened up the hose line and almost knocked him off the bike. When everybody stopped laughing, we knew was time to grab the towels clean up the mess.

"IT COULD HAVE BEEN WORSE"

Rescue 2 had just cleared from a call in the east end of our territory when we saw a column of smoke rising near the border of the City of Miami's coverage area. We put ourselves on the call and heard Squrt 2 and Engine 7 do the same and headed east. When we arrived at the front of a large warehouse with heavy black smoke and flame coming from the roof, a City of Miami engine company was already stretching a line. One of their Rescue crews appeared to be bunkered out and getting ready to go in but instead of wearing fire gloves, two of the crew had put on latex rubber gloves as if expecting to perform patient care. I saw this as an opportunity to steal their call, and we jumped in front of them to assist their engine company. They made no attempt to get to the hose line or even looked pissed that we took their call. This is by no means a slam at the City of Miami, as many rescue companies working for different organizations, including some working for Miami-Dade Fire Rescue, looked at patient care as their primary job and firefighting as something they would prefer to leave to suppression crews.

We helped pull the line and were at the front door getting ready to make entry with the crew from Miami when suddenly decorative brick and pieces of the parapet wall began raining down on us. One of the City's master streams had been turned onto the structure, but the driver/operator either did not see us through the smoke or hear his engine company communicating our position.

Master streams are either ground-based or in this case, an elevated aerial stream with a straight-stream pattern delivering about 500 gallons, or about two tons of water every minute. Normally, master streams are used in defensive operations due to the potential for injury when personnel are on the fire ground.

We dodged a bullet, so to speak, as the debris fell on us but the entire wall didn't collapse all at once. The adrenaline was pumping, and at the time we didn't realize how much of the wall had come down. We were on the call for another hour or so, and when we cleared, our necks and upper bodies starting feeling sore. By the next day, some of us were heavily bruised and black and blue but luckily, no broken bones. There were no hard feelings: it was just one of the hazards of the job.

"WRONG PLACE AT THE WRONG TIME"

22nd Avenue varies from a four to six-lane road separated by a median that runs north south for approximately 12 miles through the pleasantly named areas of Miami Gardens, Opa Locka, Westview, West Little River, and Gladeview. The top speed limit was 40 mph, similar to many other roadways that divided suburban areas across the country. Unfortunately, with major intersections only every few miles, most commuters would push the limit to well over 55 mph, and in some instances, over 70. Inevitably, we ran on hundreds of single and multi-vehicle accidents resulting in everything from minor dents to those with multiple fatalities.

In one of the more serious incidents, a driver had broken down due to mechanical problems with his vehicle. Two of his passengers got out of the car and attempted to push it to a service station or off the main road. It was just after dusk, visibility was limited, the car's electric system was compromised and had no four-way flashers or other reflective properties. The driver of a car traveling in excess of 60 mph didn't see the vehicle being pushed, or the two soon-to-be victims. They were both wearing dark pants and were hunched over the back of the car, partially obscuring their torsos and heads. When the second car hit them, the devastation was almost immediate. The impact amputated both legs of one victim and one leg of the other. When we arrived, the victims were lying on the ground but since they were struck with such force, at least two of the legs were imbedded in the grill. One of the victims died on the scene, but the other was taken to the Trauma Center along with the driver that hit them. Another rescue crew had the dubious distinction of having to dislodge the amputated legs from the grill and transporting them to the hospital for possible re-implantation. As they didn't know which leg belonged to the survivor, all three legs were taken to the hospital.

"CAT-SCAN HELMET"

As I stated in a previous section about headache removers, some of our regulars felt it was their God-given right to call Fire Rescue for a ride to the hospital complex, whether they needed it or not. One of those frequent flyers would call approximately twice a week and had been repeatedly cleared by the doctors at JMH as having no physical ailments but a growing host of mental issues. One of his favorite problems was a creature that had burrowed into his brain (a la the Ceti Eel larvae in the second Star Trek movie) and was affecting his thought process (Star Trek, 1982).

As it so happened, we had come into possession of a metal pith helmet, most notably seen in the old safari movies designed to keep the sun off the explorer's heads. We affixed several electrodes to the helmet and once again attached them to the Lifepak. The helmet was placed on the patient and we went to work. Conveniently, the 'brain waves' we saw on the EKG monitor showed no signs of Ceti Eel larvae or any other organism in his skull. He was very appreciative when we said he appeared to have been cured. This lasted until he called us again about a week later.

"MOTHER AND CHILD LOST PART II"

Another bad accident we ran on was a 24-year-old pregnant woman who was a victim of a hit and run driver. When we arrived, she had been partially ejected through the sunroof of her vehicle, but somehow got twisted over and around and back into the passenger window in a lethally unnatural position. Due to some obvious deformities, it looked as if her neck and back had been fractured. Her skin was already mottled from severe blood loss, and she appeared to have died on impact or soon after.

A large crowd had already begun to gather and started to express concerns as to why we weren't transporting her. Someone who had evidently seen it on TV, said we should put her in the Traumahawk, a combination Police/Fire Rescue helicopter used by Broward County, approximately 30 miles north of the accident scene. Then the resultant racially-tinged commentary began such as that if she wasn't Black, we'd already have transported her. We did our best to ignore the comments and assisted police in securing what was now a crime scene, covering the body with a blue tarp to keep the onlookers from gawking.

We thought we were done with the call, but about four hours later, we were called back to the scene after the police had completed their investigation. They couldn't remove the body due to rigor mortis setting in and needed our assistance. To get her out, we had to cut through the roof slowly and carefully to avoid causing additional bodily harm, all while working under the tarp to preserve her dignity.

"HE DIED WITH A SMILE ON HIS FACE"

Early one morning we were in Station 7 when we heard what sounded like an explosion in front of the station. We ran outside and did a doubletake before we realized what had just occurred. Directly across the street was a Mazda repair shop, with several work bays at the north end of the building, and dozens of vehicles that were being worked on parked at the south end of the lot. With the exception of the gated entrance, the entire lot had a three-foot high concrete block wall with a chain link fence anchored into it, and an additional run of concertina wire atop the fence to minimize break-ins. There was a huge cloud of smoke making it difficult to see what had happened, but when we got closer, we saw that a car had hit the block wall, catapulted upward into the fencing and on top of several of the tightly parked vehicles. Sections of the block wall, some pieces weighing several hundred pounds had been hurled clear across the entire lot into the building, breaking off segments of the structure and partially crushing one of the bay doors.

After making our way across the entangled fencing, car parts and fluids spilling from the vehicles, we were able to pry open one of the doors and found two victims, one male and one female, both obviously deceased. We also found what appeared to be dozens of one-dollar bills strewn across the car and around the crash site. We couldn't figure out what was going on until our law enforcement brethren showed up with an explanation.

Looked like an explosion.

Apparently, the female worked at one of the local "gentlemen's clubs" a few miles away, and the male in the driver's seat was a customer who left with her when the establishment closed. What ensued afterward was the apparent inability of the driver to avoid pressing the accelerator to the floorboard when his companion was providing additional services not offered at the strip club.

The results of the investigation showed that the vehicle was traveling in excess of 100 mph when it made contact with the wall and fence. Talk about coming and going at the same time!

Difficult to believe it was caused by a single car.

"HE NEVER FELT A THING"

A call came in for a single car accident with a report of the vehicle striking a building. After racing to the scene, we found a car that made contact with the corner of a storefront at what seemed to be no more than 15-20 mph, a very survivable accident. As we pulled past the car to block traffic from the rear, there appeared to be minimal damage but we could see someone in the driver's seat partially slumped over. When we opened the driver's side door, we found an unconscious white male in his 20's with a needle sticking out of his arm and a spoon on the seat next to him.

What was also highly visible was a severely angulated cervical spine. It seemed that after shooting up while at a traffic light, he started to lose bodily function and control when the heroin kicked in. This caused him to be extremely relaxed to the point where the impact of the car with the building was sufficient to break his neck and kill him.

What bothered me more than anything was the lack of concern for anyone else on the road. This individual was shooting up while driving and could have easily killed another driver or pedestrian instead of just killing himself.

"DRIVE BY SHOPPING AT SEARS"

NW North River Drive at one point runs diagonally along the Miami River and has a considerable amount of commercial vehicular traffic, especially during normal working hours. Numerous shipping-related and businesses supporting the industry are located along this stretch, and the road is a direct route from two other major surface streets. A multi-vehicle accident was reported one morning around the midpoint on North River Drive between these two roads.

When we arrived, we found a tractor-trailer with its swing rear doors open and locked, parked on the right side of the road. Another tractor-trailer obviously involved in the accident was a hundred yards or so further down the road with its flashers on. The first trailer was empty but there was something not quite right. Along the inside of the trailer on the driver's side was what appeared to be a large Sears' sign. At first glance, it seemed that the trailer was carrying the sign but we realized that it was not a sign but actually part of the other truck. Apparently, the truck parked on the side of the road was not on level ground and was leaning into the roadway. When the Sears truck passed the parked vehicle, the right side of the trailer came into contact with it, literally peeling off the entire logo from the outside of the Sears truck. The driver of the first truck was in his vehicle during the accident and had his window open. Luckily, he had his arm inside the cab as the truck that passed also took off his rear-view mirror.

When interviewed, he said the truck was no more than one foot away from his face and he could feel the wind as it passed. He had no injuries but we assumed he did have to replace his uniform and underwear when it was over.

You can't make this up!

"BICYCLE VS. CAR: CAR ALWAYS WINS"

At times, you wonder what someone was thinking or in reality, not thinking when he or she make what turns out to be a less than intelligent decision that at times ends their life. Cars and trucks on the road are required to use headlights and taillights at night for better visibility, both to see and be seen. Florida law always has required bike riders to follow the rules of the road that licensed vehicle drivers have to obey. They're to stay in a marked lane or if none, as close to the right-hand curb or edge of the road as possible for their own safety. I can't say when it was first enacted, but the law also requires riders to have a white light on the front of the bike and a red light or reflector on the rear when traveling after dark.

With that said, why would a 17-year-old ride a bike down the middle of a relatively busy avenue at three o'clock in the morning with no reflectors, no lights, and to make matters worse, wear dark pants and dark shirt, making him virtually invisible to traffic until they're right on top of him? By the time we arrived, he was dead, wrapped around the bike with obvious spinal injuries and multiple extremity fractures. The first car hit him, left the scene, the second one ran him over and stopped. The only saving grace was that he was most likely killed on impact.

"NEWS FLASH"

Located in the north-central section of Miami-Dade County, the city of Opa-Locka is an out-of-the-ordinary municipality. I describe it that way for multiple reasons. It was founded by Glenn Curtiss (Glenn Curtis Museum, 2017), an adrenaline junkie and renowned motor-cycle racer and builder in the early 1900s who had a thing for Middle Eastern architecture. What's more, he was famous as an aviator and earned the title of the "Father of American Naval Aviation." Although Curtiss built an airport in the city he created, neither the airport nor a single street is named after him. He does have a parkway named for him in Miami Springs, a neighboring town that he also helped to establish. Miami Springs has no springs, but did have an Arabian-style hotel built by Curtiss; confused yet?

Here's more. The development of Opa-Locka was originally based on a collection of stories better known as the Arabian Nights. Roads within the city have names like Sultan Avenue, Ali Baba Avenue, Sesame Street, and Shaharazad Avenue. However, according to the city's website (The Great City of Opa-Locka, 2006), Opa-Locka is a contraction of the Seminole Indian word, Opatishawockalocka, which means big island covered with many trees and swamps. You guessed it: Opa-Locka is not an island, although it may have been a swamp at one time. Other exotic Arabian names such as Vermont Street, Burlington, and Atlantic Avenues crisscross the city, adding to the sham ambiance. The city has the largest collection of Moorish architecture in the country, and multiple government buildings including City Hall have domes and minarets. Railroad tracks virtually bisect the city and unless you're familiar with the layout of the surface streets and railroad crossings, it's easy to get lost or miss a turn when trying to get to a fire or medical call.

A minor fire ostensibly started in the office of a newsprint and paper supply company in the industrial section of the city. Instead of calling 911 first, the employees tried to extinguish the blaze as many are wont to do, and it quickly spread to the connected warehouse.

It was a typical hot, sunny South Florida day, and by the time they did call 911, the fire had raced through the multiple stacks of paper products in the warehouse. Hot embers were pushed through the open bay doors by the 10-15 mph breeze and landed on dozens of one-ton rolls of newsprint stacked three high in an open storage area. The rolls were being loaded onto carriers for distribution but were highly flammable due to the adhesives used in processing the paper.

As the company had been burglarized on several occasions, they parked multiple tractor-trailers end-to-end to use as security barriers, which effectively blocked much of our access to the buildings. The first arriving units could only get as close as 600 feet away so we had to hand-stretch five-inch hose. A 50-foot section of dry five-inch hose weighs around 110 lbs., and a lay of 600 feet weighs over 1,300 lbs. Each of us dragged two sections of the five-inch and made the connections as we moved closer to the fire. Other units were unable to get into the property due to the proximity of the train tracks and distance to the crossings.

Although we look closer, we're 10 feet away from the fence and out of the collapse zone.

By the time the trailers were moved and we could get additional suppression units close to the fireground, we were almost 30 minutes into the firefight. The Incident Commander decided to change from an offensive to defensive operation and protect the exposures and the remaining rolls of newsprint. Several hours later when the fire was out, we found the remains of what were originally hose cabinets. With the exception of the nozzles that were fused solid due to the extreme heat, there was no sign of the hoses or the aluminum cabinet in which they were stored. It was if they never existed.

"THAT'S WHAT FRIENDS ARE FOR"

At one time, there was a pizza takeout restaurant in one of the more dangerous sections of Liberty City. The food was good and drew people from outside the area, as far away as Miami Springs, about four physical miles away, but light years in terms of economic status. Another Friday night, another shooting. When we arrived, we found a dead customer who was a regular from Miami Springs, one of the employees wounded, and a dead teenager about half-block away, arms above his head, shirt pulled up, and pants partially pulled off.

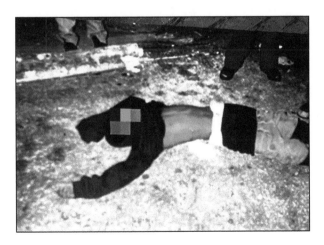

Left for dead by his "friends".

Apparently, the teen and two of his buddies decided to rob the pizzeria, and for good measure, shoot and kill the only customer. The owner pulled his own gun and shot the perpetrator, but one of his employees was wounded in the exchange of gunfire. The two surviving gunmen dragged their buddy out of the storefront by the arms and tried to get him to their getaway car. They made it about 25 feet when it appears that they heard police sirens, decided to drop him on the sidewalk and make a run for it. According to witnesses, one of them turned and came back to him while he lay dying and ripped the gold chains from around his neck. I guess they figured he wouldn't have a use for them anymore.

"TRAUMATIC AMPUTATION"

South Florida is no different from many other areas across the country in that there are multiple manufacturing plants for industries that produce and ship goods both nationwide and abroad. The difference being is that many of the workers in our area are Green Card holders; individuals who have been granted authorization to live and work in the United States on a permanent basis. Some are sponsored by family members or employers, while others gain residency status through refugee or political asylum programs. Others are on work visas, provided by the federal government to non-citizens to be able to stay in the U.S. for a limited period of time. A good portion of these workers from Central and South America and the Caribbean are unskilled, have limited educations, and are willing to take tedious or menial jobs that many of our citizens choose to avoid. Others may have entered the country illegally for economic or political reasons.

Many of these manufacturing plants utilize machines that grind, tear, shred or rip materials as part of their recycling process. Most companies abide by the Occupational Safety and Health Administration (OSHA) Act of 1970, designed to assure safe and healthful working conditions, but accidents will and do happen.

One of those incidents occurred when one of the above-described workers was feeding material into a machine designed to grab the textile fabric and rip it to shreds. It appeared that he got too close to the three-pronged claws and it caught his hand. Each ensuing claw worked its way up his arm, tearing skin and flesh, and breaking bones. This was not a rapid-fire process that was over in a few seconds. On the contrary, it was slow enough that he probably felt every point of the claw that penetrated his skin and every break of the bones in his forearm. His co-workers were frozen in fear and no one moved to hit the emergency stop button. By the time one of the other line workers snapped out of it and was able to unplug the machine, he had lost his arm to midway above the elbow. When we arrived, the patient was on his back on the floor, his skin almost white, and a vacant look in his eyes. The stump of his arm was being held up and covered with a rag by the same co-worker who shut down the machine.

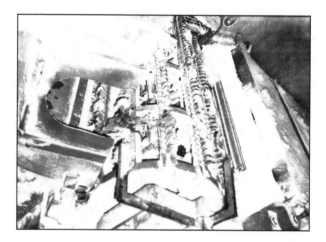

His fingers still in the machine.

Interestingly, traumatic amputations may have little or no bleeding, much less than would be expected with a wound as severe as this.

One of two things may occur. The process of hemostasis or clotting, or vasoconstriction, the temporary constriction of blood vessels which slows down or stop blood flow.

We quickly cleaned and wrapped the stump. While my crew started an IV, gave him oxygen and loaded him into the back of the Rescue, I looked around for any part of the arm that could possibly be saved and reattached. The area around his workspace looked like a scene straight out of a low-budget horror movie. Blood and pieces of soft tissue were everywhere: the floor, the claws on the machine, and imbedded in the ceiling 20 feet overhead. There was absolutely nothing to save.

"HOME ALONE"

Every once in a while, we'd run a call that would just, to put it in simple terms, piss us off. One of my pet peeves has always been children who were ignored by their parents or considered to be a hindrance to their party lifestyle. Occasionally, we'd find toddlers, two or three years old, wandering the street without a responsible adult watching out for them. My rule was simple. Pick the kids up in the rescue and take them to the nearest police station. If parents actually realized their child was missing and went to PD, I'd hope they would pay the price. Unfortunately, the penalties were rarely as severe as the offense. I understand that some people can't afford sitters or have a limited or no family support system, but if you choose to bring a child into this world, he or she is your responsibility until they are eighteen. With that said, the following shows the worst of what can happen when a child is left unattended.

We received a call for a fire out. Typically, it's rubbish or another minor fire that has usually been extinguished prior to calling 911. This practice is definitely not recommended as many times these fires quickly get out of control. The apartment complex where this incident occurred was very well-known to both fire and police. The complex was called Silver Blue Lakes, the type of name that conjures up an idyllic scene straight out of a travel magazine.

In reality, it was a three-story, L-shaped development with several connected buildings built on the outskirts of a rock pit, a large whole dug for fill that quickly filled up with water due to the shallow water table in South Florida. Rock pits differed from lakes as they suddenly drop off from the bank to sometimes as deep as 30 feet or more. Silver Blue was famous within the northern districts of the fire department for the multitude of kids who drowned in its dark, weed-filled waters each year, but those are stories to be told at another time.

Note the soot line on the walls.

In this case, the fire was on the second floor. The door was locked, the windows black from soot, but when we touched the door and the windows, they felt warm but not hot. A neighbor had called after she came home and complained about something burning or the smell of smoke. We easily made entry and saw that there a fire had been burning for a while as the smoke had banked down to about three feet off the floor. A soot line could be seen around the entire apartment at that height, and the fire self-extinguished when it ran out of oxygen. Next to the couch, we saw a shape that could have been and should have been nothing more than a pile of clothes. As we moved closer, we realized that it was a small child, possibly three or four years old who had succumbed to smoke inhalation. There was no point in working him; he had been dead for hours and the only reason he wasn't cold as ice was the residual heat in the apartment. If he was older and was more aware, he could have survived by staying low to the ground. Smoke naturally rises: if he could have crawled on his hands and knees, he would have made it to the door. However, he wasn't, and he didn't. He was a three-year old who was left home alone for some ungodly reason and paid the ultimate price.

"BABY ONE MORE TIME"

As I said, obstetrics never was my favorite subject. Having graduated from the JMH School of Nursing, working as both an EMT and RN in a local hospital emergency department for almost 15 years, and working in a lower socio-economic area for almost two decades, I was involved in close to 350 deliveries. Most of the deliveries in the field occurred because the mother waited until the last minute to call 911. Many of those young mothers had no pre-natal care, and the pre-hospital care they received from paramedics was the first time they were seen by anyone with medical training. The youngest mother I saw in the street was 13 years old, although we had an 11-year-old give birth when I was in nursing school. I did my best to educate pregnant women whenever we were on a call about the dangers of not seeing an OB-GYN or delivering in the back of a rescue but for the most part, it really was a lost cause. With that, here are two short accounts about babies we delivered.

"RESCUINA"

Having worked in Liberty City and the surrounding areas for close to 20 years provided the opportunity to see almost anything you could imagine and then some. Many of the stories have already been recounted, but when you run on frequent flyers, things happen that make you shake your head. I can't remember the specifics of this particular call, but I do remember a woman approaching us with a huge smile on her face. She apparently remembered me from a year earlier when we delivered her baby girl and transported her to JMH. She was so thankful for what we had done that she decided to name the baby after us. Since there were no female paramedics on the crew that day and she couldn't remember any of our names, she named her daughter "Rescuina", after the entire rescue crew. I didn't know if I should laugh or cry.

"YOU DELIVERED THE MOM"

Another day, another delivery; this was the call that made me decide that I had spent way too much time on rescue and needed a change of scenery. We responded to yet another childbirth in the projects and when we arrived found the mother in labor, the soon-to-be grandmother all of 31 years-old by her side, along with at least three other pregnant girls of various ages waiting their turn. Grandma looks at me and proudly says, "I know you! You delivered my baby 15 years ago and now you're delivering my grandbaby! This is my second grandchild!" I had now been there long enough to deliver newborns for two consecutive generations of the same family. The realization set in that I had been there much longer than I expected.

"MERRY CHRISTMAS"

Report of a gas line explosion and fire; not the everyday call that you get dispatched to, but the one that makes you move that much faster to the truck. All the while considering among other things, the number of victims, especially since it was Christmas Eve, how you'll manage the incident, what resources you'll need, and which units are responding. Since the call was three territories away, we were cancelled but as we were only a few blocks away at the time, we continued to roll in. As we turned the corner, we saw a column of flame 25-30 feet high near a drilling rig. A company had been hired to drill holes near a concrete slab to install a utility pole, and the crew that consisted of an operator and his son-in-law were trying to finish the job to meet a deadline. As it was the holidays, one or both of the workers were enjoying some adult beverages; not the best of recipes when combined with operating heavy machinery. Needless to say, they either misread the site plans identifying where the gas line was located, it was not properly marked, or the alcohol affected their judgment. They ruptured the underground one-inch diameter, high-pressure gas line, releasing flammable gas that came in contact with an ignition source which most likely was the drill bit coming in contact with the gas line. The fire was so hot that we could feel the radiant heat almost 100 feet away. The resulting explosion and fireball killed the operator and sent his son-in-law to the hospital. Merry Christmas.

"SUICIDE BY HANGING"

It's sometimes hard to understand why people do what they do. Many of us go about our daily life without a second thought to those around us. We do our jobs and don't want to know or become involved in the trials and tribulations of others living in our community. South Florida is an amalgam of people from across the Americas, the Caribbean, and places beyond. However, that doesn't necessarily make it easy for them to adapt to the American way of life.

What a way to go.

Of the thousands of calls that I ran on, some left indelible marks on my brain. One of those I wondered about for years was why a 91-year-old would hang himself in his backyard. The call came in as a man down; a vague reference that could mean almost anything. When we arrived, we saw an older man facing away from us who appeared to be kneeling on the ground next to a tree. As we approached him, I realized that his neck appeared slightly elongated and he had a small rope wrapped around his neck and tied to a branch above him. At first, we couldn't see the rope as it was obscured by a garden hose that was also hanging from the tree. He literally was on his knees at that point, but it makes you realize that whatever demons possessed this man made him hang himself using nothing but his body weight.

"HOLDING HANDS"

Station 2 and 7's primary response zones are in two zip codes, 33142 and 33147. At last count, there were almost 500 "official" churches in those areas. This doesn't include the dozens of storefront churches that don't have websites, aren't listed on search engines, or provide services for a very small following. I firmly believe that these two zip codes have more churches per capita than anywhere else in the County, probably the State, and I would venture to say, the country. Gospel churches, especially in the Black community in the 1980s drew huge numbers of worshippers. Every Sunday, we could count on at least two or three responses to neighborhood churches, usually with a respiratory or cardiac origin.

This call came in as a possible cardiac arrest. Rescue 7 and Engine 7 were dispatched, and Rescue 30 was clearing from a call and responded with us. On arrival, we found a 72-year-old woman in cardiac arrest and immediately started CPR. While two of the crew-members alternated performing compressions, others were setting up IVs, getting ready to intubate, and charging the defibrillator to shock her. Just as they put the paddles on her and were about to send 300 joules or units of energy coursing through her body, I realized that at least 10 other elderly women were in a line all holding hands with one another and with the patient and praying. I can't tell you if the shock would have affected all, some, or none of them, but I definitely had no intentions of finding out. As soon as I saw the daisy chain of worshippers, I yelled at my guys to stop. We separated the ladies, continued with treatment, and transported the patient to the hospital.

"DON'T EAT THE CRUMB COFFEE CAKE"

Every so often on a Sunday morning, we would go to a well-known national bakery chain store that sold day-old baked goods. Day-old is no big deal, but back then was a considerable cost-savings when buying for eight or more people. It's the same food you find in a supermarket chain but there was a stigma attached to the fact that it wasn't considered "fresh." Nowadays, the food is used in recipes, donated to food banks, or in some cases, still is sold at outlets. This particular outlet was always extremely clean, had a good safety record, and friendly, dedicated employees. However, accidents do happen, especially around large baking machines like dough mixers.

One of the bakers was adding crumb coffee cake ingredients to the mixer and caught his index finger between the edge of the bowl and the spinning dough hook. It took off the distal phalanx, or tip of the finger cleanly. It wasn't what we would consider a major injury, but there would be an obvious difference of opinion with the individual who lost the digit. Nonetheless, the reason for having included this section is that the fingertip, complete with bits of bone, flesh and blood was fed into the system that would have ended up as tasty coffee crumb cake. I'm sure that by law, the machine was shut down, cleaned and inspected before going back in service, but just to be on the safe side, we avoided coffee crumb cake for a couple of months.

"RECOVERY, NOT RESCUE"

For the most part, I love the cops that we worked with day in, and day out, and have total respect for them and their profession. They are intelligent, street-smart, dedicated men and women who many times give more to the public than is deserved, including their lives. Sometimes however, just like in the fire service, one or two do slip through the hiring process and you think to yourself, is he serious or just putting us on? They definitely have no business wearing the uniform and should be working in an office setting where they won't hurt themselves or others.

Case in point; we were in route to a call for a routine sick male when we heard the dispatcher announce a second call in our territory for a possible drowning in Silver Blue Lake, police on the scene. We took ourselves off the routine call, made a U-turn and jumped the drowning call, which was about three miles away.

Miami-Dade Fire Rescue has the largest rescue dive program in the world. With over 1,000 rock pits and lakes, 300 plus miles of coastline, 1,500 miles of inland canals, and an average of 40 drowning deaths every year, the need for rescue divers has always been there.

My crew and I were all rescue divers. I jumped in the back with the third medic and both of us started donning our SCUBA gear in order to be ready to go in the water when we arrived. We came out of the back of the truck fully dressed out with swim fins in hand, looking for the victim.

What's referred to as a floater.

One of the police officers who we knew slowly approached us and with a sheepish look on his face, mouthed, "I'm sorry." Apparently, his supervisor who was new to the area but was very impressed with his new Lieutenant's badge, directed him to request our presence. It seemed he had a case of heavy badge syndrome, which means that on occasion, new officers, both Fire and Police, become overly impressed with themselves and the authority that supposedly comes with the position. The Lieutenant wanted us to go in the water to retrieve a body about 100 yards offshore. I asked for a pair of binoculars and saw the body that appeared bloated due to gases building inside the body cavity, causing it to become buoyant and ride high in the water.

I could also see blood-soaked areas on the shirt and decided that since we weren't wearing wetsuits and there appeared to be a considerable sheen on the water around the body which could be bodily fluids, neither I nor my partner were going in the water. This wasn't a rescue mission and the health hazards were too high.

To save some time and effort on the part of MDPD's underwater recovery unit, I advised the Lieutenant to bring their helicopter that was circling overhead down to about 30 feet above the surface and use the downwash from the rotors to push the body back to shore. Once they were in place, this took about 15 seconds. The body had been in the water for several days and appeared to have at least 11 bullet wounds in the back.

I asked the Lieutenant for a moment of his time and proceeded to chew his ass professionally for misusing resources and not giving a damn about putting our personnel in jeopardy. This was accomplished in private but it was clear to everyone else on the scene as to what was happening. His mouth dropped open and at first started to become indignant, but quickly changed his tune when his District Major who I had known for almost 20 years showed up and bro-hugged me.

"FETAL DEMISE"

The south end of our territory was comprised of multiple sections of middle-class single-family homes with quaint names like Pinewood, Brownsville, and Earlington Heights. There was a mix of duplexes, triplexes, quadraplexes, apartment complexes and multi-family public housing projects. In our territory, some of what were originally designed and built as single-family homes were turned into rooming houses without the benefit of an inspection. They were then subdivided into as many as five or six separate living quarters where there would normally be only one. Hot plates or Sterno cooking fuel that served as kitchens were next to the beds, and the single bathroom in the house was shared as many as 10 adults, and at times, kids. Octopus connections, or multiple extension cords were used to increase the number of electrical outlets through a single circuit or socket, and cords were run under through rugs to avoid trip hazards. Each of the interior rooms had a hasp and a padlock that the occupants had to lock whenever they left the premises or the room would be emptied when they returned. Just a fire or disaster waiting to happen.

Then there were the crack houses. Ramshackle structures without electricity or water, many previously abandoned by the owners due to economic setbacks, then broken into and occupied by squatters, usually druggies. Crackheads would turn tricks on old mattresses they found in dumpsters and dragged back to the crack house to make a dollar to buy more drugs. Their heroin-addicted friends would occasionally join them. Needles, razor blades and piles of garbage and human feces were everywhere, and during the summer, the stench was incredible.

Typical crack house.

Normally crackheads are easy to spot. Their fingertips or lips are blackened or burned from holding the hot crack pipe until they've smoked the last bit of cocaine. They are severely lacking in personal hygiene, and their anxiety borders on paranoia. Once they ran out of coke, they would start to freak out and call 911 for everything under the sun.

Just another view.

The public knows 911 is for emergencies, but the abuse and misuse of the system by the drug subculture was, and still is rampant. Calls like "I've been constipated for three months and want to go to the hospital"; I have a wart on my hand since last winter;" or "I've had a headache for seven years" (no joke, they all really took place).

After a while, you start to downplay every call that comes out of one of these places. When we were called for a woman feeling sick, our first thoughts were, here we go again. On arrival, it turns out she had abdominal pain and vaginal bleeding. While we were attending to her, one of her roommates walked up and said that just before we arrived, she threw something out the window. I sent one of my crew outside, figuring it was drugs that she didn't want found on or around her. My partner returned with something completely different: a recently deceased fetus that the patient had aborted and tossed out the window. We transported her with a police escort to Ward "D."

"MUTANT AVENUE"

One of the areas we responded to on a regular basis was a three-block stretch we called Mutant Avenue. We named it for good reason; actually, way too many good reasons. For the two dozen or so single-family homes on this avenue, we had responded to at least 80 percent of them from medical calls to domestic disturbances to house fires. I swear that inbreeding was rampant, as most of the children looked like they had the same Neanderthal brow.

One of our frequent flyers was a woman in her 70's who claimed to have respiratory problems and would call 911 an average of two to three times a week. It doesn't sound like a lot until you realize that we ran on her for almost 10 years, and the other two shifts probably saw her as much as we did. She did have asthma, but I think we only had to transport her once or twice when she was much older. The source of her discomfort emanated from her two sons who lived with her. Both were in their early 40's when we first encountered the family. The brothers were subject matter experts in recreational drugs and wine that primarily came with screw-off tops. It didn't take long for them to experience the long-term effects of substance abuse. All three were heavy smokers, and the mother usually had a cigarette in her hand when she called 911. The two sons always wore baseball caps, and their long scraggly gray hair would hang almost to their shoulders.

They constantly fought with one another, many times leading to fisti-cuffs, and both constantly fought with their mother.

In 1990 in Gainesville, home of the University of Florida, four female and one male student were murdered and horribly mutilated by a serial killer. It made national news and put everyone on edge. A few days later, we responded to their home once again with the mother complaining of difficulty breathing. However, when we arrived, there was something perceptibly different. One of my partners slowly glanced up and saw literally dozens of wig heads on the shelves around the living room. Each of the heads had multiple scars drawn on the faces and most of the scars had stitches drawn on them. As we stared at the heads, one of the brothers said, "Scary huh? Just like Gainesville!" We reported it to the police who said they'd broken no laws but would definitely keep an eye on them.

"ALL PROFIT"

Nearly everyone knew that Miami was the cocaine capital of the world in the late 80s and early 90s. Marijuana and heroin as well as millions of dollars in illicit drug money also flowed through Liberty City and the surrounding areas like the canals that crisscrossed the County. Many saw the drugs and fast cash as their way up and out, but very few made it out except by way of the Medical Examiner.

On any given day, you would see cars that by themselves were virtually worthless but were unbelievably tricked out. Some had thousands of dollars' worth of Trues (Truespokes, a brand of wire wheels) and Vogues (whitewall tires) that were worth dozens of time more than the cars themselves. Many also named their cars with overtones of wealth, the fast life or an overinflated self-image.

Early one morning around 02:00 hours (always seemed to be after midnight), we were called for a possible shooting in the projects. A bronze-colored, mid-size, convertible pickup truck (more drug money spent wisely) had pulled up to a railroad crossing and was waiting for one of the Florida East Coast Railway trains to pass. The trains that passed through were anywhere from 50 to 90 cars long and would always be at that crossing at roughly the same time each night, traveling at a relatively slow rate of speed. Somebody else was aware of this and knew their target either was not, or thought he was untouchable.

He had no chance.

The first car pulled up behind him and slammed into his bumper so he could not escape, and a second pulled alongside. The occupants of both vehicles started shooting, killing him almost immediately. According to witnesses, the whole episode took less than two minutes. The acrid smell of gunpowder was still heavy in the air when we arrived with police within three minutes of getting the call.

Although it was a crime scene, they either neglected to fully cover the body or someone on-scene pulled the sheet off him. This almost caused a riot as dozens of family members and friends had shown up and were in the street at the time. There were at least 17 bullet wounds in the body and dozens of additional holes in the car. As it was a convertible, his body was visible to almost everyone in the immediate area.

The local media had already shown up. One of the South Florida stations that shall remain nameless had the reputation as nothing more than an on-the-air tabloid, and favored showing people at their worst, especially those in emotional or physical distress. When one of the wannabee fourth estate morons reached across a "Do Not Cross" scene tape and stuck his microphone in a family member's face to ask how he felt, his response was a fist to the reporter's jaw, knocking him to the ground. The "journalist" looked at me for help with fear in his eyes. I shrugged my shoulders and gave him a you asked for it glare. I mentioned earlier that many of these cars had names; this one was ALL PROFIT. Based on the final outcome, it looks like his rate of return went into the loss column.

"DOWN TIME"

On days when the dispatchers were slammed and the radio was burning up with calls, there was no point in going back to the station as it could delay our response to the next run. Once we cleared a call, we'd occasionally cruise through the neighborhoods and projects trying to identify either new businesses or construction (extremely rare), or recently abandoned structures that were prone to arson.

Bobby Flintroy used to catch snakes and iguanas and sell them to pet stores, and occasionally would tell us to stop near one of the overgrown lots. For the uninitiated, iguanas are one of the many non-native species that have called South Florida home since being introduced into our local ecosystem by escaping from or being released by pet owners. The green iguana which is native to the Caribbean, Central America and the warmer climes of South America, can grow to over five feet in length and weigh close to 20 pounds. Outside the U.S. they are known as 'pollo de los árboles,' or chicken of the trees and are considered a dietary staple. As their popularity as a food source increases, U.S., restaurants and customers are paying trappers up to $60.00 a pound for iguana meat.

That being said, Joe Sollecito and I would sit on the back bumper of the rescue listening to our handheld radios and tell Bobby that he had ten minutes, no more. It was a wonder to behold; the big guy jumping into the weeds and repeatedly, coming up with a three or four-foot iguana or five-foot yellow rat snake.

Looks worse than it is!

On another foray one morning while passing through one of the local trailer parks, we found an abandoned mobile home. Someone had started burning trash in a 20 x 30-foot-long hole next to the trailer. We called for one of the suppression units to put the fire out, but while we were waiting, we saw a chance for a unique photo opportunity.

With a big smile on his face, Flintroy climbed into the hole and positioned himself away from the fire. From our vantage point, it looked like he was surrounded by flames. The engine crew did a double take when they saw him until they realized he was laughing at them.

"HALF A CHEESE SANDWICH"

It's sad how little respect many people have for the elderly. A lack of respect can at times become neglect, and more often than not, neglect becomes abuse. In our society, parents are expected to be the primary caregivers for their offspring. The roles should be reversed when the parents are older or need assistance and the children are grown, but that's not always a reality. Unfortunately, I've seen way too many parents dumped in South Florida by their affluent children who live elsewhere, many times several states away.

In this case, multiple generations of one family lived with an elderly man who was the patriarch of the family. The call came in as a routine response for a sick male. It definitely was no emergency on the family's part as when we arrived as they continued to watch TV and simply pointed to the back bedroom.

Walking down the hallway, we turned into a small bedroom and with a look of disbelief, realized that lying on a bed was an elderly man, naked, barely conscious and covered with ants. He had been bitten hundreds of times. We quickly brushed off as many as we could, pulled the bed sheets off him and found him to be cold to the touch. Then I noticed something on the nightstand: a half a cheese sandwich and a glass of milk. There was no way he could have possibly picked it up on his own, let alone eat it. I thought it could be a case of elderly abuse so I quickly took a picture of him for the police.

Ants were everywhere; hundreds more were in the bed with the patient, nesting under him. We cut open two bags of saline to wash the remaining insects off him, grabbed the sheet off our stretcher and wrapped him in it.

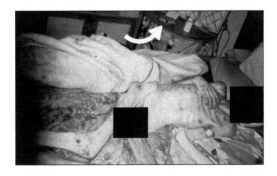

It would be impossible for him to have eaten this (arrow) without help.

As we were rushing out of the house to get him to Jackson Hospital, the family actually had the audacity to ask if he was alright. There was no emotion, just matter of fact. It seemed that the last time anyone even spoke to him was weeks or months earlier. While in route, we did what we could, but he was so emaciated we couldn't start an IV. We gave him oxygen, covered him with several blankets to keep him warm but really nothing more. We called ahead to the hospital and they had an isolation room ready for him. The nurses at Jackson had seen everything under the sun but they were horrified and livid at seeing this little old man. After multiple attempts, they were able to start a line to give him fluids. Regrettably it wasn't enough; he died two hours later. The photo was used as evidence in court against several of the family members, and at least two were convicted of neglect and served jail time.

"LEECH DIVING"

Although we live in South Florida, we do have what we conveniently refer to as cold weather. There are actually times when the temperature can drop into the 50s and even the 40s. It doesn't last more than a day or two, but it's not typical South Florida weather. As we in the fire service know, things don't happen on nice sunny days when conditions are ideal. They happen in February at 03:00 hours in a near-freezing rain in a canal covered with algae.

The call came in for a possible drowning in Opa-Locka. The Rescue at Station 26 was on another call and we were dispatched to respond with Aerial 26. Police were on the scene and advised that a passerby (it's always a passerby) saw a man on the side of the canal bank with a pair of crutches and when he went by again, the man was gone and one crutch was lying on the bank. The initial assumption was that the man fell in the water and had possibly drowned. The canal was covered with blue-green algae, aka cyanobacteria, which grows into a large expanse called a bloom. A large bloom covered the canal with no sign of a break. That told us that there was very little chance of anyone having fallen in the water in the past 30 minutes or so.

Now, common sense would normally prevail, but we're not paid to make decisions that could cost someone their life. We're paid to go the extra step and take chances. Based upon that minimal amount of information provided to us on-scene, Bobby Schneider and I went through the algae into the water in just shorts, a t-shirt and SCUBA gear. The water was about 70 degrees, which doesn't sound bad until you're in it without a wetsuit. After 20 minutes or so, we had completed a linear search. We found the other crutch in the water, but no victim. As we climbed out of the water, the rest of the firefighters realized that we were covered with leeches. We stripped everything off as quickly as could and the aerial crew started pouring isopropyl alcohol on us and pulling the leeches off one at a time. The middle of the night in a street in Opa-Locka, naked, freezing, and worrying about leeches is not my idea of a good time.

We didn't know it then, but fresh water leeches live in relatively slow moving or calm water such as canal banks and are not really harmful to humans. They are also found in murky water making them harder to see. They are called Haemophagic (bloodsucking), attach themselves to the host (us) and release an anesthetic, which is why we didn't feel them when they bit us. It seems that they don't do any lasting damage but when you become a "Happy Meal", that's the last thing on your mind.

It turns out the guy with the crutches was looking to pawn them off and figured they were worthless. He had thrown them on the ground and one fell into the water, leading to our unnecessary search and rescue mission.

"AN ELECTRIFYING SITUATION"

No matter what you learn in Fire College or during on the job training, there are situations that arise that will constantly surprise you. If you're not paying attention, it could be easily become your last call. A simple "possible smell of smoke" call, one that we were dispatched on hundreds of times, required an entire house assignment to roll in. We were first in and knocked on the door multiple times, yelling "fire department, anybody home?" and never received an answer. Although there were no signs of fire, the smell of a burning ballast was present. Based on that information, we had no choice but to make entry.

The apartment had a backdoor with jalousie panes. As previously noted, jalousies were glass slats in metal frames that were part of the South Florida flavor. As exterior doors on residences, they let in light, and when the slats were opened, allowed the breeze to circulate freely throughout the structure. They were big in the 50s and 60s in Florida before air-conditioning became omnipresent, and many of them actually survived into the latter part of the century. They were also extremely easy to break into, as the occupant of this apartment found out on several occasions.

Just as we started to make entry, one of the police officers yelled for us to stop. He said he had responded to this residence on both real and suspected break-ins multiple times, and the inhabitant had threatened to electrocute the next guy who tried to rob him. Before moving forward, we had the electric company come out to shut down the power to the entire apartment complex. Once that was accomplished, we pried open the jalousie door and found what the cop had predicted. An extension cord had been plugged into a wall socket with the insulation stripped off the female end. One wire was attached to the metal frame around the jalousies and the other wrapped around the screw to the doorknob. Had one of us touched the doorknob barehanded, we would have possibly gotten an unwanted surprise.

Under normal circumstances, firefighters should be relatively safe from the effects of 120 volts of electricity if they are fully bunkered out with structural firefighting gloves. However, when sweating under that gear, your skin's electrical resistance drops dramatically. The amount of current that goes through the body goes up when the resistance goes down. The current may not kill you but it will definitely get your attention.

"GOOFY DRESSING"

Alcohol, drugs, and overcrowding are a dangerous combination. Add weapons and egos to the mix and things can go downhill fast. Assaults were commonplace, with head injuries ranging from contusions and lacerations, to gray matter splattered all over the sidewalk. For the minor injuries, we'd cover the wound with gauze 4" x 4" s and wrap their head with kling. For the occasional characters who continued to mouth off as to how badass they were and would take care of the guy who just whipped their butt or those who would be escorted to jail, we wrapped the kling around their heads, leaving large open loops hanging from both sides of their head that resembled Goofy's long floppy ears.

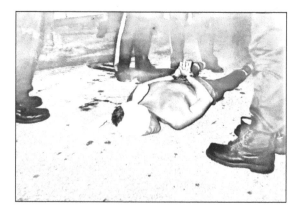

You won't see this at a theme park!

If anyone questioned what we were doing, we simply explained that it was easier to remove the bandaging with the large loops in place. For one particular bad boy who was under arrest, cuffed and on the ground on his belly, we added a special touch by wrapping the kling over his eyes as well. He continued to talk trash about his opponent and threaten retribution as soon as he was released.

"DON'T BRING A KNIFE TO A GUNFIGHT"

In addition to the innumerable assaults we saw almost daily, armed robberies were also fairly common. Usually the target was someone who wouldn't or couldn't fight back: the elderly, the infirmed, women with children, or tourists unfamiliar with the area who would have difficulty providing a description to the police. Gold chains and bracelets, purses, wallets, and at times, even loose change was taken, even from children.

In this incident, a gunman walked into a shop near Opa-Locka and yelled for everybody to hit the floor. Several customers inside immediately complied with his instructions but for some unknown reason, one of the workers behind the counter tried his best to prevent the criminal from completing his mission. His only weapon was a 10" butcher knife, which may have been adequate had he not been behind the counter and three feet away from the gunman. He had no chance and was shot in the face and killed instantly. The gunman escaped empty-handed.

"TOURISTS TARGETED"

During the 1990s, there was what some described as an epidemic of tourists being targeted and killed. The majority of them originated in Germany, Canada, and Great Britain, and had flown into Miami International Airport before renting a car in an attempt to drive to their vacation destination. In the late 80s and early 90s, it was common for rental cars to have license plates that read "Manatee County," clearly identifying the occupants as tourists to those in the know. The reason behind this was that rental car companies received a discount when they bought the tags in Manatee County as opposed to purchasing them in South Florida. Other license plates read "Sunshine State" at the bottom or worse, "LEASE." For the bad guys, it was like putting a bull's-eye on the car.

Most of the victims were traveling to Miami Beach or Fort Lauderdale and inadvertently took the wrong exit, which at times took them to the intersection of NW 62 St. and 22nd Avenue, not exactly the safest area in town. When they pulled into the corner gas station to ask for directions, the predators were lying in wait. In other attempts, the muggers would bump their car from behind or try to get them to pull over by telling them they had a flat tire.

Over a period of approximately 14 months, almost a dozen foreign tourists were robbed and murdered. As the numbers began to rise, tourism officials had new directional signs placed along the expressway to try to guide visitors in the right direction. Unfortunately, the thugs took the signs down and the murders continued. At one point, one of the rental car companies actually posted warnings to their customers saying, "Beware of people who yell, honk or point at your car as if something is wrong, motion or ask you to stop or help them; flash their headlights or bump your car from behind. If any of these techniques occur, do not pull over or stop; instead, drive immediately to the nearest service station or well-lighted area and call the police." (Mirth and Madness, 1998).

For some reason, what did not seem to make the news was a technique used by many of these dirt bags who knew that assault and battery charges would not result in life in prison or a death sentence. The 10-20-Life statute or minimum mandatory sentencing did not go into effect until 1998. When drivers realized they were about to be robbed and refused to open their windows or unlock their doors, the criminals would swing spark plugs tied to strings into the side windows. The windows would shatter, stunning the driver or passenger and the mugger would reach in, stealing their purse or valuables.

Eventually, the powers that be realized that if they didn't put a stop to this, the economy would suffer (naturally the main concern). Bringing the attacks to an end was made a priority, and local law enforcement were able to take most of the predators off the streets.

"SEEING IT FROM BOTH SIDES"

Having worked in a hospital Emergency Department (ED) as both an EMT and RN for 16 years, I have a tremendous amount of respect for hospital-based personnel, especially registered nurses working in the ED. From the minute they show up at work, it's an almost non-stop onslaught of patients. Breaks are virtually non-existent and are considered a luxury. It's a highly stressful environment with an almost continuous flow of patients brought in by fire rescue and private ambulances. Adding to the controlled chaos are the steady stream of walk-ins with complaints from flu-type symptoms to a full-blown cardiac arrest arriving in the family vehicle.

On the other hand, those working in the hospital setting are at times oblivious to the conditions in which pre-hospital caregivers have to operate. Firefighter/paramedics or EMTs work accident scenes in lightning-illuminated thunderstorms, contaminated environments, or under adverse conditions that require but don't always have a police presence. We've intubated patients who were hoarders, still sitting in their recliners while one of us was wedged behind them standing up. They couldn't be lowered to the floor to as stacks of their accumulated possessions barely allowed us access to them to begin with, and the likelihood of these items falling on the patient were a real possibility.

Having worked both sides of the fence, I felt it was necessary to ensure that both Fire Rescue and hospital personnel had a better understanding of what went on in each other's workplace. In the early 90s, we offered to have some of the RNs occasionally ride with us which they accepted and also proposed to schedule some of the medics to complete an eight-hour shift per month in one of the local EDs. It was an eye-opener for many and for a short time, a greater respect for each other's jobs. As normally occurs, people move on or move up and expectations changed.

In one case, we had a seven-year old girl who was hit by a car, run over, and dragged for more than a block before the driver left her there to die. When we arrived, she wasn't breathing and we could clearly distinguish tire tracks running diagonally across her chest. We wasted no time and immediately got her in the back of Rescue 2. The Lieutenant on Squrt 2 and both of his firefighters who were also paramedics jumped in the back with us to help work her. While in route, we tried everything we could to save her. I told our driver that we were not secured and to try to let us know when he was turning or braking so we wouldn't get slammed into one of the cabinets or each other. We were able to get one IV started and intubated her while CPR was being performed.

When we arrived at JMH, they rushed her into one of the trauma rooms, but her injuries were too massive and she was pronounced dead. While we were cleaning up, one of the nurses came out of the trauma room and started making remarks in front of her co-workers about how the child wasn't intubated properly, and why couldn't these firefighters do their jobs like they're paid to do, blah, blah, blah. I overheard her comments and they sent me over the edge. Seven of us were working in a four by eight-foot box moving at 60 mph and putting our lives at risk for this child that for all practical purposes had no chance. Apparently, the endotracheal tube had slipped out, either when moving the child from the stretcher to the hospital bed or bouncing in and out of multiple potholes in route to the hospital. The trauma surgeon also heard her comments and looked directly at her telling all of us that if it weren't for us, she would have had no chance at all. The nurse turned red and apologized, saying it was in the heat of the moment and uncalled for. Apology accepted, on to the next call.

"UNDER THE INFLUENCE"

State Road 112, a six-lane expressway that runs east west for almost 10 miles, divided our territory. On the north side, the clientele was mostly Black while on the south, they were predominantly Hispanic, with many from Central America. The southeast end of our territory bordered on the City of Miami and was home to several low-rent trailer parks that catered to illegal immigrants. Like every other neighborhood, more often than not, the residents of the parks were good people just trying to get by, but they had to deal with a smattering of morons and petty criminals.

A popular pastime of those who couldn't afford much else was to drink. Any alcoholic beverage at a reasonable price would suffice, but there were clear favorites. Malt liquors, fine wines such as Thunderbird and MD 20-20, and Popov Vodka were preferred. Some of our customers held their liquor much better than others. With one consumer in particular, when the sun went down, so did the booze.

Good Samaritans driving by one of the trailer parks would periodically call 911, saying there was an unconscious man on the ground. Other times, a concerned resident would call, saying she wanted him to stop vomiting in front of her kids. Once we heard the trailer park address, we were 99 percent sure who we were running on. We would find him passed out, sometimes on the sidewalk, and at times, literally face down in the street. It was amazing that he was never run over. Two or three nights a week, we would get the cops to help us carry him a few feet away from the street so he could sleep it off in the bushes.

We knew he frequented a local bar about a block away that was popular with illegal immigrants. It was owned, or at least operated by someone who had also come from somewhere in Central America. We happened to be driving back from JMH one night and I told my partner, Robert Gaitan, that we were going to cut the number of calls we ran on this guy in half. He gave me a half-smile and asked what I had planned. I told Robert just to follow my lead and translate everything I said as closely as possible. We parked in the gas station diagonally from the bar and walked across the street. Two men in uniforms with badges and handheld radios walking into a bar full of illegal aliens brings about a strangely quiet atmosphere.

As we watched several of them slowly move to the rear exit and leave, I told Robert to ask for the owner. The man was hesitant to come over to us but he really had no choice. I told him in English and Robert translated into Spanish that if anyone left his bar and was hit by a car, we'd have Building and Zoning close his bar and report him to the police as an accessory to a crime. We had absolutely no authority and it meant nothing, but the word "policia" was enough to make him do exactly as we asked. We rarely saw our friend after that.

"FIELD TRIP"

A bus full of elementary school children were excited to go on their first field trip of the summer. They, along with their chaperones were headed southbound on 27th Avenue and were in the left lane stopped at a red light. In the right lane next to the bus was a flatbed truck carrying a load of steel I-beams. They were stacked three-high, secured, and appropriate warning flags attached to the back of the beams that hung off the back of the truck. However, as the truck started to make a right turn at the intersection, the overhanging beams at the top of the stack swung wide to the left, hitting the back of the bus and cutting through the windows and side crash rails like soft butter.

Dozens of kids could have been killed or severely injured.

The children at the rear of the bus on the impacted side were knocked down like bowling pins. Those too short to be hit by the beams as well as the kids on the opposite side were hit by flying glass and pieces of metal. By the time the truck driver realized what was happening, the beams had cut through half of the bus. At least eight children had been injured, ranging from minor cuts and abrasions to two with serious head injuries. They were transported to the trauma center and luckily, all survived making a full recovery.

"FIELD PROMOTION"

In almost 20 years at Stations 2 and 7, we estimated that we saw over 1,800 student riders. These were observers from other departments, EMT and Paramedic students from various local colleges and for-profit schools completing ride time, as well as newly hired personnel assigned to us during part of their probationary periods. Most of the probies were very respectful and kept their distance, but some mistook friendliness in the professional setting to mean we were their long-lost friends.

In public safety and especially in the fire service, you make yourself invisible and small until called upon to participate (see Rookie's Introduction to Station Life). One probationary firefighter in particular at Station 2 mistakenly understood our taking him under our wing as the right to jump into conversations that didn't involve him, and to become sarcastic and challenge senior personnel: a right that was earned with time in grade, not bestowed upon you by virtue of simply wearing the silver badge. He even went as far as to violate one of the unwritten laws of the station by sitting in the front row of recliners, which were designated for senior personnel.

One day, his bravado got the best of him. He was close to my size and about 20 years younger, but I had the wealth of experience, was much stronger, and most importantly, had the element of surprise. He started in by saying something like, "Cap, you're pretty solid but

I was in the military and have a martial arts background" (generally, when someone brags about martial arts, they talk a big game but have not made it a lifetime pursuit). "I think you and I should go a few rounds." He was smiling and certainly meant no disrespect, but you don't challenge your officers unless you're willing to be put in your place, or to put your officer on the spot, which he did. I told him, "Be careful what you ask for, you may get it." Of course, he started to reply, "bring it on." By the time he finished the word 'it', I had already bum-rushed him.

He was standing in the dayroom with his back about a foot away from one of the filing cabinets, and unfortunately for him, was only four feet away from me. Law enforcement officers will tell you that it takes roughly 1.3 seconds for an attacker to move 21 feet. His mouth was open and the look of surprise on his face was priceless. Before he had a chance to lift his arms to defend himself, I put him in a front headlock. I squeezed him for about 30 seconds and when I released him, we saw the imprint of two crossed bugles on the left side of his forehead. Apparently, I had him in a perfect position against my badge pinned to my jumpsuit.

Everyone burst out laughing, and like a gracious prizefighter who had just been defeated, he acknowledged that he had been beaten by the better man. He also confessed that he didn't think I could move as fast as I did considering I was almost 50 at the time. I saw him periodically over the years and am happy to say that his level of maturity grew by leaps and bounds. We became friendly and before I retired, he had been promoted to Captain, and is now a Battalion Chief.

"DRIVING IN MIAMI"

South Florida, and more specifically Miami and the surrounding municipalities are not known for their driver's safety records and politesse. The region is a mishmash of South Florida natives, retirees, and both legal and illegal immigrants. In many Caribbean, Central and South American countries where these immigrants originate, there is a severe lack of decorum in sharing the road.

We seem to have more than our fair share of drunk drivers, hit and runs, and seemingly magnetized pedestrians and bicyclists who draw vehicles off the streets onto the sidewalks, into bus stops or into their two-wheelers. Individuals who have had their licenses suspended or revoked have a conveniently short memory and are found behind the wheel on a daily basis. Some believe that the Department of Motor Vehicle's point system is a contest to see who can score the most, and many others have never bothered to take the driving test at all. I won't even talk about texting or cell phone use. That's another book by itself.

As an example, we had one gentleman who was so focused on getting from Point A to Point B that nothing, including several cars stopped at red lights or legally parked in front of their homes were going to slow him from his appointed rounds. According to witnesses, he sideswiped the first parked car and continued for almost five blocks before hitting the second and third cars. By this time, several other civilian drivers were in pursuit, trying to stop him. Remember that cell phones were not the norm and calls to 911 had to be made through landlines, resulting in a delayed police response.

He continued on for at least another mile before he rear-ended another car pushing it into the intersection where two more vehicles inadvertently joined the fray. Multiple Miami-Dade officers as well as police from a neighboring municipality were on the scene by this time and had the individual handcuffed when we arrived. Amazingly, no one was injured although over a dozen vehicles were involved in the accident.

"SAVE THE WABBIT"

Another day, another house fire: we quickly got it under control and completed a primary search. When the smoke began to clear, we realized that inside the house was a menagerie of both domesticated and wild animals. There were dozens of snakes, lizards, a couple of chickens and several rabbits, all of which had died from smoke inhalation.

Bobby Flintroy, our reptile specialist was bothered by the number of animals that had perished, especially the snakes. As we were making our way out of the house, he said, "I think that rabbit just moved." I asked, "are you sure?" He responded, "no, but I think it may be alive." I told him it was up to him if he wanted to work it. He picked the rabbit up and as he started walking outside, he said, "I think it's dead." Too late: as he stepped into the light, the decision to work the rabbit was made for him.

As soon as he moved outside, one of the local television stations stuck a camera and a microphone in his face and asked if the rabbit was alive. Before he had a chance to reply, I told the reported that this intrepid firefighter would do his best to save the poor little bunny. He gave me this look of disdain but walked over to the back of the rescue cradling the rabbit in his arms. As soon as he laid it down, several other firefighters walked over to help. They grabbed the limp rabbit, began administering blow-by oxygen and considering we had no training regarding the anatomy of a rabbit, did their best to perform

CPR. In the meantime, Flintroy set up for an endotracheal intubation using a pediatric ET tube.

Meanwhile, the cameraman from the station had positioned himself over one of the firefighter's shoulders forcing them to work on the animal under even more pressure. We on the other hand were standing back and enjoying this immensely. We egged them on by telling the reporter that if anyone could save the rabbit, he could. They worked on the animal for almost twenty minutes before calling it quits.

It turned out that the rabbit was the pet of a six-year old girl who was heartbroken that her little Fluffy had died. We felt bad about her losing her pet, and as a group, we decided to chip in to buy a new bunny for the little girl. The original story made the news and somehow our Public Information Officer got wind of our idea and wanted to film the event. We weren't looking for any recognition but it was too late: we were directed to make it a full-blown presentation.

We bought the replacement rabbit at a pet store and tried to find one that looked like the one that died. We thought it would be most appropriate for Bobby to be the one to give the rabbit to the little girl. When the big moment arrived, he took it out of the cage and held it close to him. Right then the rabbit decided to sink its teeth into Bobby's hand. Although the bite drew blood, he remained composed and he slowly walked over to the girl. The rabbit continued to bite him and made him visibly wince.

All I could think of was that the cute little bunny would tear into the little girl and our good deed would become a public relations nightmare. As he handed the rabbit over to the girl, we collectively held our breath. She cuddled the bunny in her arms and the rabbit actually looked happy. We cleaned up the blood and wrapped Flintroy's hand so he could wave goodbye to his cottontail vampire.

"WHEELCHAIR BOUND"

We had what seemed to be more than our fair share of individuals relegated to wheelchairs. They were there for multiple reasons, but more than a few were paraplegics secondary to being shot. Others were homeless and had various ailments, most of which did not require the use of a wheelchair but was definitely more convenient when looking for sympathy when panhandling.

Several would not come out until darkness fell, hanging out with their compatriots on one of the street corners. Some of them would ingest so much alcohol that they would pass out or in some cases, literally slide out of their wheelchairs. Late into the night, people driving by would see them lying on the sidewalk or in an empty lot and of course, call 911.

We would arrive, help them back into their wheelchairs and usually get a second call for them a couple of hours later. Bringing them to an emergency department was not the answer. On the contrary, it would have been a disservice to the ED staffs to dump a chronic alcoholic on them just to sleep it off.

Explaining why they shouldn't drink and try to sleep it off in public fell on deaf ears. In order to prevent seeing our habitual offenders several times in one night, we would tie them into their wheelchairs with a bed sheet and roll them of the beaten path to get a night's rest. Occasionally, one or two would insist on sleeping under the bright lights of 27th Avenue and like a crocodile's homing instinct, would find their way back, only to have us called out again. For those who couldn't control themselves, we would push their wheelchairs to an area out of sight of the main road that had sugar sand and bury their wheels to keep them busy for a few hours. Most mornings at the end of the shift, we would go by to check on them but they would be long gone.

"RECIPES FROM HELL"

Unless you have one of those rare individuals who epitomize what the firehouse cook is about, most stations ask that everyone takes their turn in their barrel so to speak and cook one meal every three weeks. When I first I got to Battalion 5 and more specifically Firehouse 2, I was asked if I had a specialty. I couldn't boil water without burning it but for some reason, my mouth opened and the word, "ravioli" fell out. I remembered seeing frozen ravioli with directions on how to cook them in an Italian market in the north end of the County, but for some reason, the guys thought I meant I could cook them from scratch. When it was my day and I brought the frozen ravioli in, I got some looks but no comments.

Dinnertime. I opened the boxes, started to follow the directions and was actually proud of myself for getting that far. Unfortunately, there were no directions on what to do if you have to stop cooking and go to a warehouse fire. I turned the burner off, covered the pot and ran to the truck. I didn't think anything of it, even when we cleared that call and went to a house fire...and then another house fire.

Five hours later, we got back to the station. I uncovered the ravioli which had morphed into some sort of pasta soup. I scooped out what I could salvage, put it in the microwave, and served it with dried out garlic bread placed around the soup to form a retaining wall. For some reason, I was not allowed to cook again for seven years.

Here are some of the other "favorites" that I and several other "chefs" concocted. I won't throw the others under the bus but they know who they are. The first few were mine: Side of Beef Stir-Fry, in which I mistakenly purchased stew meat thinking it would work for beef stir-fry. It didn't. Meatloaf Mountain: I made 10 lbs. of meatloaf for seven people and it was barely enough. Meat Logs (shaped like you-know-what with fennel (looks like grass) and kernel corn and served in miniature plastic toilets. The next two can be attributed to my partners: Everything is Baked Ziti (anything Italian, call it Ziti), and Galvanized Chicken, where you could literally bounce a chicken leg off the floor and catch it. Some others that are clearly self-explanatory and speak for themselves: Chicken Chernobyl, Rice Pudding Plaster, Terra Cotta Mexican Tile Brownies, and of course, Cat Litter Cake. All recipes available upon request. One of Chief Mike Simon's favorite sayings was, "This is food fit for a King. Here King, here King."

"BACKDRAFT"

One of the primary reasons for many fire-related calls coming in late at night or in the early morning hours is that if it was a commercial structure, it was most likely unoccupied after business hours, allowing the fire to grow. It was also easier for arsonists to do what they want when no one was around as this was long before security cameras and systems were widely used. If it was a residence, the occupants were probably sleeping and did not recognize the danger signs until much later, sometimes a little too late.

A call came in for light smoke coming from a restaurant across from the Miami-Dade College North Campus. The restaurant was located directly across from one of their main parking lots, separated by a six-lane thoroughfare and median almost 10 feet wide.

We were about two blocks away when we saw debris fly out of the building and blown almost completely across the street. It was a little eerie as there was no sound; nothing that would indicate there had been an explosion. As we drove past to set up Command and allow the engine better access, we realized that all the front windows had been blown out. Once the fire was extinguished, we could see broken glass, canned goods, food, and silverware strewn across the road. We walked the length of the debris field and found items from the restaurant that had been blown almost 100 feet away and realized that we had missed being in the blast of a backdraft by just a few seconds.

"SINGLES ONLY"

On one particularly busy morning, Gary Pilger initially shelled out the money to cover dinner for the crews. Later that night when dinner was over, I collected five dollars from everyone in order to pay him back. On one of those rare occasions, it turned out that everyone had put five one-dollar bills on the table. Before Gary could collect the money, the engine crew was called out for a dumpster fire.

In a sudden moment of clarity, I thought it would be a great idea to line the bills up end to end and scotch tape them together. I then carefully folded each one over the other so that it appeared to be a stack of neatly arranged one-dollar bills. To add to the illusion, I folded the bills in half and tied a rubber-banded around them. When Gary and the engine crew returned, I threw him the money, which he pocketed without looking at it.

There was absolutely no need to count the bills as we all trusted each other as brothers and sisters. Firefighters may steal your food or your girlfriend, but you could leave $1,000 in cash in the table and unless someone broke in, it would be there when you came back. Nothing was said, and at the end of the shift, we left to go about our business. After returning to the station the following shift and finally sitting down to breakfast, Gary told us that he had gone to one of the local grocery stores his first off-duty day and when he reached the checkout line, pulled the wad of bills out of his pocket to pay for his groceries.

When he started to peel off a dozen or so singles, the wad unraveled into a conga line of cash. There were several people behind him in line and they and the cashier stared at him as if he had antennae growing out of his forehead. He gave them a wry smile and said, "Sorry, firefighter humor."

"COMPLACENCY"

After two decades of working in Operations and all but three months of that part of my career in Liberty City, I started to become complacent on calls; not burned out, but complacent. I don't believe in burn out. I think that's a cop out for people who don't want to work in certain areas of the community or run a lot of calls. Most major urban departments are large enough to offer both lateral and upward moves by those who think they've been in one place too long.

I started to notice that complacency on trauma calls. I wasn't getting the adrenaline rush that usually came as soon as the dispatcher announced the call. One of the definitions of complacency is a feeling of quiet pleasure or security, often while unaware of some potential danger. When you become complacent, you start to lose your edge and keen sense of surroundings, which can lead to you or someone else getting hurt. It's important especially as a supervisor to remain calm, but you should be all eyes and ears in order to protect yourself and your crew.

I first noticed it on a domestic violence call with the husband, wife, several cops and my crew in an apartment living room no bigger than 10' x 14'. I was near the wall but not touching it. We had two unwritten rules when going into someone's home. One was not to sit on furniture. Your uniform may be dirtier than you realize and you're not a guest, you're there to provide a service. Then again, the furnishings may not be as clean as you'd hope. The second was a variation of the first: never lean against a wall as the home may not be as clean as you are and this avoids, or at least minimizes cockroaches, rats and other vermin from crawling on you.

I was writing my report when the wife grabbed a butcher knife from under a cushion. The cops quickly took the knife away and calmed her down but she immediately grabbed a second, larger one from behind a cabinet. This time she came a little too close and I had to deflect her and the weapon with my metal clipboard. The cops grabbed and cuffed her and I went back to finishing my report. A search of the house found four more knives conveniently placed for future use. Similar situations occurred on other trauma calls and I began to notice that the only thing that got me worked up was a fire: otherwise the excitement of running the calls was slowly waning. What I also realized was that the constant pounding on my knees from jumping off the truck with 40-50 lbs. of gear was taking a toll on my knees. It was time to take the Chief Fire Officer exam.

"TOO YOUNG, TOO FAST"

The shift before I took the Chief Fire Officer (CFO) test was fairly typical for Station 2, around 20-25 calls for the shift and five after midnight. With the exception of the previous weekend, I hadn't studied so I had no great expectations. I didn't expect to do well so I wasn't overly concerned about taking the test after being up all night. The last call of the night came in around 04:00 hours as a single-car accident with only Rescue 2 dispatched. While in route, it was upgraded to an overturned vehicle, but since we would be there in less than 30 seconds, I held off on having the Squrt roll with us.

Upon arrival, we found a partially overturned minivan that had hit a telephone pole at a high rate of speed. While my crew was pulling equipment for a possible extrication, I did a quick walk-around to ensure that the area was safe and that we didn't have any ejected patients in the immediate area. I saw one, then two extremities, at different angles sticking out of the demolished van. I called for the Squrt and an additional rescue which was Rescue 7. I realized that there were at least three victims inside if not more. I asked for the Battalion Chief and a TRT unit to assist with the extrication.

While they were being dispatched, we started to try to get to the victims. I say try, because there was a total of five: three dead and two that were still alive but trapped underneath the deceased. I directed the Squrt crew to stabilize the vehicle in order to allow us to get inside to work on the victims. We quickly realized that the way the car had wrapped itself around the pole and the fact that the positions of their friend's bodies were making it extremely difficult for at least one of them to breathe. This could cause a significant delay in extricating them quickly and safely.

The Lieutenant assigned to the TRT unit and I decided that since one of the legs of one of the dead twenty-somethings had been partially severed, we needed to cut through the remaining tissue and bone to get to one of the victims underneath to give her space to breathe. We used trauma shears to cut quickly through the tissue that was still attached, and bolt cutters to get through the shattered bone. By doing so, we were able to provide supplemental oxygen to the girl underneath her dead friend. By this time, we had four rescues, two Squrts, an engine, and a Battalion Chief on the scene, with a total of 25 personnel working the call. As we extricated the surviving victims one by one, we turned them over for transport to the trauma center.

It was now after 07:00 hours, and the "B" shift crews were on-duty. The lieutenant that was relieving me drove his own pickup truck to the scene and let me take it back to the station to get to the CFO test in time. Before I left, I briefed him as to what we had done and what still needed to be accomplished. He gave the keys to his truck; I gave him my hand-held radio still splattered with blood and I flew back to the station. I showered, finished my paperwork and made it to the test with about seven minutes to spare.

After completing the test, I headed home to get some well-earned sleep. As I waited at a red light, it suddenly dawned on me that at least four probationary firefighters were working on various units on the call. Recruits had a blue crescent on their helmets that clearly identified them to others on medical or fire scenes. As this may have been the first major trauma call they had ever dealt with, the mental anguish over working kids their own age may have been more than they could handle.

I realized I had to call for a Critical Incident Stress Debriefing (CISD) that at the time was commonly used to mitigate the effects of stress associated with a traumatic event. When the debriefing was held the following shift, most of those who were on the call were in attendance. What I didn't expect was that many of our personnel who had been on the job for four or five years identified with the victims, more so than the probies. I learned something new that day.

PART IV: TIMING IS EVERYTHING

"MOVING ON"

I spent almost 20 years in Battalion 5, not because I had to, but because I loved it. I felt like my career had flown by. I remember quite clearly standing in line in 1984 to pick up my first set of turnout gear which had seen significant wear and tear by those who used them before me. I loved everything about the job: the guys (generic for the men and women), the rush that came with every fire and trauma call. I had total respect for (almost) everyone that I worked with and knew they had my back every time we rolled.

I also realized that at 52 years old, I had to think about my next five to ten years in the fire service. Over one's career, the physical requirement of the job puts a significant strain on a firefighter's joints, particularly the knees and back. Every pound of body weight yields four additional pounds of force on the knee (Kane, 2011). Translation: with our bunker gear, SCBA, and other equipment weighing in at about 75 pounds, we added about an extra 300 pounds of force each time we dressed out. Going full throttle without warming up, and repeatedly jumping off the truck in all probability caused additional damage.

I couldn't handle going to a slow station; physically I was getting older, but mentally, I still thought I was a rookie. My other options were to consider a lateral move and bid a position in the Training Division, Special Operations or with any luck, become promoted to Battalion Chief.

I didn't think I had a chance to be promoted when I took the test, but apparently, the years of studying for Lieutenant and Captain paid off and by a combination of luck and osmosis, I passed. I was surprised that I scored as well as I did but the timing was such that I had already bid Engine 37 in order to be able to study for the following year's test. Engine 37 was fairly busy but couldn't compare to some of the busier suppression units across the County. In addition, I didn't think I would be promoted and expected to die on the list. As time went on, I realized that I would make Chief and had about five months before I would have to leave my new home.

"WELCOME TO FIREHOUSE 37"

When I first bid the Captain position on the engine company at Station 37, I had some misgivings about leaving Battalion 5. I had spent almost twenty years in essentially the same territory and was stepping way out of my comfort zone. I had heard the typical rumors about how difficult it was to get the crew on Engine 37 to do their job. Once I got there, I introduced myself and sat down with the crews to discuss my approach to running the station and responding to calls. Interestingly enough, the crews said they heard stories about me that scared the heck out of them but I didn't seem to be that type of person. I explained that I did nothing to dissuade the rumors about me, as I didn't want people at the firehouse who didn't want to be there.

As we went forward through the next few shifts, I started to realize that most of the rumors about the crew not wanting to be the first in on calls in their own territory traced back to the Captain I had replaced. He had a reputation for being slow to get out of the station and wanted his driver to drive slowly, using safety as an excuse. After a few fire-related calls, I could see that my driver/engineer knew his territory very well but still drove like my grandmother on sedatives. I also asked other officers about him. Each one described him as conscientious, a hard worker, and a great driver. On one particular call, he missed his turn and it was obvious that he was really upset with himself. Once we cleared the call, I told him, "Frank, I can see that you are an exceptional driver; I trust you to go as fast as you think necessary." He responded, "Really? I was directed by the other captain to go slow but I knew he didn't want to be first in." I replied simply that I trusted him. From then on until he retired a few months later, no one ever beat us to a call in our own territory.

"SOVEREIGN NATION"

At the time I bid Station 37, it was the westernmost station with territory coverage extending all the way to the county line, almost 80 miles away. One morning just after 03:00 hours, (we seemed to get many calls around this time), we cleared from a minor house fire and had pulled into the station when we got the call for a second house fire. This was almost 30 miles away from the station in the middle of the Everglades on property owned by the Miccosukee Tribes of Florida. The Miccosukee are a sovereign nation, but more on that later.

I was still new fairly to the area and started putting my gear on when my driver said, "Take your time. I'll let you know when we're about five minutes out." It's an odd feeling responding to a fire just sitting in the cab of the truck not ready to jump out and go to work. For my entire career, I had worked in urban areas and arrived at fire scenes within minutes. Finally, my driver said it was time as we were getting close. I finished dressing out, but fully expected to find a burnt-out shell of a house when we arrived.

As we turned the corner, to our surprise we saw a column of smoke and flames shooting 20 feet high through the roof. The fire had been burning for a while but because it was in an enclosed space, the oxygen content in the ambient air was reduced. It reached the point where there was insufficient oxygen; somewhere in the range from 12-16 percent, depending on the type of fuel that was present. Some fuels, especially those with high carbon content require more oxygen for combustion. If at the lower limits, the fire is deprived of oxygen and is reduced to the smoldering phase. This is the stage where the fire is nothing more than burning embers but are still extremely hot. Over the next 30 minutes or so, the embers continued to slowly burn completely through the roof, allowing oxygen to be reintroduced.

It's important to note that thanks to the visual broadcast media, in almost every fire portrayed on the big screen or on television, there's little if any smoke and usually a blazing inferno (no reference intended to the movie). This is understandable as no one would pay to see an action movie with no action on the screen.

In reality, in poorly ventilated structures or a contained smoky environment, the smoke can be so thick you literally can't see your hand in front of your face. This one looked like a fire you see on TV. As soon as we made entry, we could clearly see across the house and were able to make our way to the seat of the fire that was in a back bedroom. When the fire ventilated, smoke, heat, and toxic gases went out through the opening and were replaced with cooler, cleaner air, making it much easier to see. One of the rooms we passed in route to the fire was open and had what appeared to be multiple boxes of ammunition inside. We weren't overly concerned at first, as the room was separated from the back bedroom and not involved.

Someone had started the fire in the bedroom closet: we knocked it down quickly and continued to ventilate. We then noticed what at first glance appeared to be a sculpture in the corner of the bedroom, but then we realized it was a stack of long guns that had melted together. At the same time, one of my firefighters said, "Cap, you need to see this." He took me back to the room with the ammunition where two fully loaded Mk-19 Grenade Launchers were stored just out of sight. At that point, I ordered my personnel to leave the house as quickly as possible. We were dealing with an arson case, thousands of rounds of ammunition, explosives, and who knows what else. Discretion before valor.

Miccosukee and Miami-Dade Police were on-scene, and both Fire and Police arson investigators were in route. When we went outside, we saw members of both police departments in a heated discussion. It turned out that the home belonged to a Miccosukee law enforcement officer, his girlfriend had set the house on fire, and there had possibly been shots fired. Once it was discovered that it was one of their own, Miccosukee PD thanked the MDPD officers for their help and said they could leave. They would handle it internally.

This was a first for me; I knew that the Miccosukee were a sovereign nation, but I didn't know that they could arbitrarily decide to handle a case involving one of their own. Apparently, a federally recognized Indian tribe and a sovereign tribal government is not subject to a court's jurisdiction unless the Tribal Council consents to or waives their rights, or if Congress repeals the law. (Houghtaling v. Seminole Tribe of Florida, 611 So.2d 1235 (Fla. 1993)).

The MDPD detectives told me, "That's it. We have no choice. We're off the case." They weren't happy about it but understood the ramifications of not letting go of the case. I never heard how it turned out.

"GROW HOUSE"

In the 1990s, South Florida was the epicenter for marijuana grow houses. They were predominantly in rental properties located in residential neighborhoods, unbeknownst to families living just a few feet away. The grow house could accommodate hundreds of plants worth hundreds of thousands of dollars.

To avoid detection by neighbors, the growers would block every window with heavy curtains, newspapers, or any other opaque material. They would then revamp the interior of the house with grow lights, add fans for air circulation, cut holes in the walls and ceilings for ventilation and irrigation lines, and rewire the house, all with supplies available at your friendly local home improvement stores. To avoid further detection by the authorities, they would tap into neighbor's electric lines or go directly to the main power lines to bypass the electric meter.

For the most part during that those years, the individuals involved in marijuana trafficking out of these homes were not violent per se, but there were situations where booby traps were set. These were not so much for police and fire personnel, but as a deterrent to competitors stealing their product.

One of the multiple grow house fires we responded to was actually an explosion followed by a fire. Apparently, the entrepreneurs had used a liquid fertilizer to feed their plants under the hot grow lights.

Normally, the lower explosive limits aren't a concern, but a confined space such as an attic where external ventilation is minimal or absent, plus the empty fuel containers left in the space added to the flammable vapors. The hot lights heated one of the metal surfaces and provided the ignition source, and the result was an explosion. The pressure from the explosion caused the walls to expand and buckle, and the roof actually shifted after being separated from the ceiling joists. No one was home but we counted 141 plants that were incinerated.

"REMODELING BY FIRE"

Toward the late 1990s and into the 2000s, some of the neighborhoods in Miami, especially in the southwest section, saw a significant increase in kitchen fires. A greater percentage of the time, the fire started because a pot with some sort of food, cooking oil, grease or some other substance was left on the stove, boiled over, and ignited. This is not a new phenomenon, nor is it relegated to Miami. However, arson for profit and especially kitchen remodeling by fire was and continues to be big business in South Florida. Many of the homes in question were 20-30 years old and the homeowners wanted to upgrade, but only through their insurance carriers.

The typical pot on the stove fire is found when a family member is cooking a meal, most likely with the rest of the family still in the house, or about to return home from either school or work. In possible arson cases or suspicious fires in general, the homeowner doesn't even call 911. If we're lucky, 911 would receive a call by a concerned neighbor or passerby, usually mid-morning or early afternoon, as a smell of smoke or something burning. Conveniently, the "cook" is nowhere to be found. They had to go the store for a missing ingredient, went outside for some excuse, or were in another part of the house with an escape route should the plan go sour.

What makes it worse is that dishonest insurance claim adjusters who work with the homeowner, earn a percentage of the claim and inflate the damage estimates for a cut of the take. It's extremely difficult to prove as arson unless accelerants such as gasoline are used to speed up the process, or better, when the homeowner brags about what they did, or the adjuster is arrested for another case and incriminates everyone to receive a lesser sentence.

"SHORT-HANDED"

One afternoon, one of the firefighters on my crew had to leave suddenly for a family emergency. This left us with a three-man crew for 20-30 minutes until he could be replaced. Not five minutes after he left, a call came in for light smoke coming from a townhouse complex a few blocks away from the firehouse. We dressed out and were there in a couple of minutes.

When we arrived, fire was blowing out of the first-floor kitchen windows at almost 45 degrees and was quickly building. The crews on the next due apparatus were still clearing from another fire and were at least 10 minutes out.

Now we all know and try to follow the "Two in/Two Out Rule", but if we waited until we had backup, we'd not only lose the townhouse but both attached occupancies. More importantly, we had no idea if any of the adjoining homes were occupied.

We know that for budgetary reasons, many professional departments staff their suppression units with three firefighters and rescues with two paramedics, and unfortunately, quite a few still have two-man engine companies. However, the safety of our personnel and the public, regardless of the apparatus they ride on, should be everyone's top priority. Multiple studies by renowned organizations including the National Institute of Standards and Technology, International City Managers Association, International Association of Fire Chiefs, and the International Organization for Standardization, all recommend minimum staffing requirements of four or more personnel in order to permit effective operation of fire companies at the scene of a structure fire.

We started to flow water through the kitchen window when we heard a crash. The sliding glass doors shattered, creating a small fire tornado. The glass doors were blown across the courtyard in front of us, allowing complete access to the structure. We stepped inside over the twisted doorframe and quickly extinguished the fire. Since the other units were still four or five minutes away, we completed a search of the fire floor and then went on to search the second floor. We were also able to save some of the homeowner's personal effects, such as family photos.

The next arriving engine crew showed up just as we exited the building asking what we needed. We smiled and told them that overhaul of the fire scene was now theirs.

"NEW RESPONSIBILITIES"

As long as I have been in the fire service, I've been involved in, or overheard discussion as to which promotional opportunity is the most difficult to adjust to. Generally, the argument focuses on whether the transition from firefighter to company officer is more challenging than that from company officer to Chief Fire Officer. The first is true in that officially, one day you follow; the next, you lead. We know that there is much more to it. Multiple articles and books have been written on leadership and the challenges of exchanging the silver for the first gold badge. Leadership doesn't come in a packet along with the badge but entails a wide variety of both internal and external influences.

Moving from the firefighter position to that of company officer is "easier" in the respect that most firefighters work side-by-side with a company officer on a daily basis, and by osmosis alone, soak up a significant amount of knowledge. A good officer takes it upon him or herself not only to give direction to subordinates, but to mentor those under their command, and anyone else who is willing to listen and learn.

Earlier, I referred to learning from both good and bad officers. Like it or not, every department has both and that trend will continue in the future. Not only as officers, but especially as leaders, we must remember that not only our supervisors (and we all have them, even Fire Chiefs), our peers, and those working under us are constantly evaluating our performance. Not necessarily in writing or how we follow the rules, regulations, and policies, but how we carry ourselves, and how we interact with them and the public we serve.

With my Battalion Chief's approval, I would advise firefighters assigned to me who were either studying for the Lieutenant's exam or had already made the promotional list that they would be the Acting OIC their next duty day. If at all possible, we would review the officer responsibilities and any appropriate policies and procedures at the beginning of the shift. I would tell them up front that they would only act as the OIC until 19:00 hours unless we were running calls, and then absolutely no later than 22:00 hours. When that was completed, I would then hand the clipboard (before computer tablets were used but after the abacus) and handheld radio to the prospective officer and we would exchange places on the truck. After each run, usually on the way back to the station, we would discuss what went right, and what could have been improved on the previous call. Not surprisingly, based on my observations during that shift, I would occasionally learn something new that made me a better officer as well.

If it got a little too busy or the firefighter seemed overwhelmed, I would take over a little earlier. We would then sit down with a cup of coffee, review their reports or answer any questions. With each ensuing shift, the firefighter would get progressively more comfortable with the responsibilities of the position.

The move from Captain to Battalion Chief is a far different situation. You are moving into a position that by virtue of rank separates you from the crews, both figuratively and literally. You're no longer part of the team concept, don't ride with a crew, and wear a white button-down or polo shirt adding to the symbolic separation. Your job morphs from that of a station commander to a combination of administrator/battalion commander. In many cases, this is an exempt management position, leading to an even further disconnect.

Although you receive training and believe me, I had some of the best Battalion Chiefs in the business as mentors, there is still a significant mental adjustment. Several months later I entered the next phase of my career and was promoted to the official designation of Chief Fire Officer.

"A NEW BATTALION CHIEF"

When a Chief Fire Officer is assigned to Operations, he or she is referred to as a Battalion Chief. The promotion to Chief Fire Officer can be more than a little disconcerting for the reasons listed above. It's also a steep learning curve in the sense that many of those you previously worked side-by-side with, now eyeball you from a different perspective. For the first two weeks after being promoted, we rode with other Battalion Chiefs to learn the administrative end of the job. This in itself was more stressful than any fire call I had ever been on. I've never been a numbers guy and am dyslexic when it comes to math which added to the anxiety.

When I was first promoted, I thought I had to be more restrained in my interaction with the crews as I was concerned that everything I did or said was under the microscope which in essence, it was. One of my biggest fears was that I would screw up, make the wrong decision and end up getting one of my personnel injured or say or write the wrong thing, costing the department money or credibility. I had actually considered giving it up and go back to Captain. Fortunately, I didn't.

The assignment of Battalion Chief is a quasi-administrative position. He or she is the intermediary between the boots on the ground and management. Depending on where you work and who is under your command, the job can be extremely difficult as a few personnel come to work with the sole intent of testing every rule and regulation, or a piece of cake as others are there simply to do the job to the best of their ability. As time went on, I accepted the fact that I was there to stay and my job was to look out for my crews, both in a physical sense and administratively as well.

As I alluded to earlier, not every fire administration puts the welfare of the troops first. When you have a supportive administration and a strong labor organization, it's the best of both worlds. I was fortunate in that throughout my career, most of the Fire Chiefs I served under tried their best to do the right thing for the right reasons. There was only one who along with certain members of his command staff, seemed to make every attempt to distance themselves from those in the field. They rebuffed the uniform many of us wore proudly and opted for three-piece suits with a badge hooked on their belts. External training or educational opportunities that were sent to headquarters rarely filtered down to the personnel in the field and when they did, the time frame to register was very limited or the classes had already been filled. Divisiveness and mistrust became the rule. Thankfully, this and other questionable practices that benefitted a select few were relatively short-lived and went by the wayside when the next administration took charge.

During my time as a frontline supervisor and then as a member of management, I learned what I considered to be one of the most valuable lessons I was able to pass on to others. If personnel made an on-scene decision that didn't quite adhere to existing policies or procedures but ultimately resulted in a better patient outcome, or their thought process benefitted the community we served and not themselves, it was simple. I asked for an explanation as to why they did what they did and if they considered alternatives before coming to that decision.

Everyone makes mistakes. Anyone who says they've gone through their entire career without violating a policy or procedure is either a liar or didn't bother to consider an alternate course of action when appropriate. I told them that if they saw small flecks of feces on their shirts (figuratively speaking) they could be sure that I was covered from head-to-toe. My job was to provide my personnel with the tools and training to accomplish the task at hand and to get out of their way. As a manager, it was also to deal with any issues at the lowest possible level and implement disciplinary actions as a last resort. They also knew that this was a one-time occurrence and that they had to learn from their mistakes. Most did and became better firefighters for it as did I.

PART V: CONCLUSION

"THE CHRISTMAS TREE EFFECT"

Over the past five decades, the composition of the Fire Service has changed dramatically. What were originally organizations comprised primarily of white males have rightly become much more diverse and demographically representative of the communities that many departments serve. Thankfully, many fire-rescue departments have leaders that have come up through the ranks and are forward-thinking.

Unfortunately, what hasn't dramatically changed is the approach of some administrators within some departments, whether recently appointed or in those positions for many years. This applies to single station departments and those with personnel in the thousands. I use the term administrator as opposed to fire personnel as many of these individuals spent minimal time in, or never actually worked in Operations. Many have little or no concept of, or worse, care what front-line personnel actually do in order to protect the public. Unfortunately, they are the policy makers, or by virtue of filling a position, become self-proclaimed subject matter experts.

To add to the problem, there are numerous elected officials and self-proclaimed "authorities" who have little or no concept of the intricacies of what the fire service consists of. Many politicians, and ultimately those appointed bureaucrats working for them, are given positions of responsibility much of the time well outside their areas of expertise. These individuals are sometimes hired directly as managerial interns with the intent of developing them into department directors or city or county managers. The "mentors" assigned to guide these individuals may be department directors or assistants whose work experience was, you guessed it, graduating from similar programs and serving in the same capacity.

Most do their best to learn about their respective fire service organizations and work closely with and listen to the recommendations of the professionals in those departments. Unfortunately, others feel inclined to get involved in making strategic decisions, looking only at the bottom line as opposed to considering the complexity and risks associated with the profession of firefighter. In addition, after being elected they are generally briefed by the career professional on how that particular department operates. Miraculously, some become fire service experts by osmosis, never having even felt the heat from a fire or run a single rescue call.

These same administrators see no difference in the dangers fire-fighting brings as opposed to other occupations although studies have proven that firefighters are at greater risk than the general population for cardiac and respiratory problems, hypertension, and cancer.

Years ago, I heard a county administrator whose responsibilities at the time included our Fire, Police, Corrections and Rehabilitation, and Emergency Management departments say, "Anyone can be a Fire Chief or a Police Chief. A manager is a manager no matter where they work". I vehemently disagree.

Many true public safety officials have decades of hands-on experience and formal education commensurate with overseeing public safety, but they also know that providing direction to the troops means more than just following the book. In order to best enable and to support those under your command, it is critical that a fire service administrator at any level has served in the positions they manage. An administrator should be operationally competent in all areas, but particularly when supervising those specialties that require certification. At the very least, administrators should attend and successfully complete command level courses specific to that area of expertise.

First and foremost, to properly understand the role of firefighter and officer, it takes time in grade, and practice, practice, practice. As the saying goes, "you're only as good as your last call". This also translates to those working in an administrative setting. You're only as good as the last decision you made to support personnel working in Operations. Everything within the fire service exists to support Operations, whether it's Communications, Logistics, Fire Prevention, Training or any of the specialty areas. Without our core mission, those areas would have no reason to exist. Many of us realized that the only way to change the culture was to become part of it.

Where am I going with this? It leads me to discuss those who subscribe to the organizational principles of what I refer to as, "The Christmas Tree Effect". The average table of organization in any business is similar in shape to that of a Christmas tree. There's only one position at the very top, and as you work your way down the branches, more and more positions appear; some necessary, some superfluous. There are two types of ornaments; those made of crystal, glass, porcelain or other fragile materials, and those that are handmade. The first are delicate and breakable, expensive to make and hard to replace. The fragile ornaments are highly visible, positioned either near the top or conspicuously placed on the front of the tree for maximum visibility. The latter are handmade, of wood or other types of workable materials which take time, effort and love to create. They generally have imperfections from being handmade or carved, worth little except to those who created them and those they were given to. Most fill space at the bottom and sides of the tree or are used to cover the open spaces between the branches, hardly visible to those who come to admire its overall beauty.

The goal of the fragile ornament is to sit alone atop the tree; or to be the most visible in the front of the tree close to the top where people will ooh and aah over its beauty and perfection. The handmade ornaments gradually increase in value, both sentimental and financial. The scars and scratches received in those early years become less and less visible, but have a history associated with them that the more fragile ornaments could not have weathered. They are sometimes handed down through the generations and cared for and admired as their strength and beauty grows over the years. Meanwhile, many of the fragile ornaments break, simply from having the stress of being packed away or put on the tree again and again.

The fragile ornaments near the top of the fire service tree, whether sworn or civilian, are often comprised of those who have either met the criteria of being in the right place at the right time, a special assignment that goes on much longer than originally expected, and was, or knew someone who was politically connected. The fragile ornaments also have a tendency not to share information with others or to surround themselves with top-quality personnel. This comes from a fear that their weaknesses or lack of knowledge would be exposed or that someone would take their job. The fire service succeeds not because of, but in spite of these individuals.

How do we correct this? Start by requiring people hired as fire-fighters to work as firefighters, nothing more. No administrative jobs, no long-term restricted-duty, no special assignment. No one should be allowed to take a promotional exam without having completed a minimum of five consecutive years as a firefighter working in operations or in a directly-related support role. Probationary periods should be extended if a firefighter has passed probation and goes out on restricted duty for any reason; medical, psychological or emotional.

Miami-Dade Fire Rescue currently requires that a firefighter must serve at that rank for five years prior to taking a promotional exam. However, the rule only applied to five years on the job, not actually working in the position originally hired for. This was not a departmental decision: instead, it was mandated by County policy-makers who had never set foot on a fireground. There are very few departments in this country that provide the number of calls necessary to ensure the knowledge, skills, and ability to lead by example with five years on, let alone less time on the job. Regardless of what many "experts" claim, the occupation of firefighter has been and will continue to be one of the most dangerous jobs in this country.

Periodically, I would encourage young Chief Fire Officers and Captains who worked their way through Operations to take the next step and become part of their administrations that so many seem to disdain or to become leaders in their respective labor organizations. I advised them that they only had two choices; consider leaving Operations to replace those actual leaders retiring from staff positions and move the department forward, learn both what to do and what not to do, or step aside and allow the fragile ornaments that are waiting in the wings who will surely take charge if they don't. Unfortunately, many of those officers believe that labor organizations are the only means to redress any inequities committed by incompetent administrators or worse, those with personal agendas. As I said earlier, a strong labor organization is necessary to ensure that an administration looks out for the well-being of its personnel, especially when the administration in power does not necessarily consider that to be the top priority.

Mentoring in the fire service, especially when the economy takes a downturn, is difficult to justify, but essential to ensuring continuity and passing years of accumulated knowledge to the new leadership. Allowing personnel with that vast amount of experience to leave the fire service without sharing their knowledge and experience is a travesty. It not only hurts the department but the public as well. Many in the service who are respected by their peers and supervisors for their knowledge base are willing to share that knowledge and mentor others simply if asked.

Tomorrow's leaders are those handmade ornaments; handmade by leaders in the fire service who are willing to recognize their abilities, enabling them to complete tasks and assignments by supporting them, encouraging them, communicating with them, motivating them, and rewarding performance, not necessarily through compensation and/ or benefits, but by recognizing their accomplishments and showing appreciation, especially in a public setting.

REFERENCES

Angulo, R. (2012). Fire Apparatus Magazine. *Iron men and wooden ladders*, Retrieved from: http://www.fireapparatusmagazine.com/articles/print/ volume-17/issue-2/departments/tool-tech/iron-men-and-wooden-ladders.html

Croker, E. F. (1910). Fire Museum of New York. *Firefighter heroism quotes from history.* Retrieved from: http://www.firemuseumnetwork.org/ misc/quotes.html

Darmon N, Drewnowski A. *Contribution of food prices and diet cost to socio-economic disparities in diet quality and health: A systematic review and analysis.* Nutr Rev. 2015;73:643-660.

Duncan, C. (2008). About Santeria, Retrieved from http://www.aboutsan-teria.com/what-is-santeria.html

Firefighter's Cancer Foundation (2018). Retrieved from: http://www. ffcancer.org/?zone=/unionactive/view_article.cfm&HomeID=27469 7&page=Cancer20Research

Florida Fish and Wildlife Conservation Commission (FWC, 2018). *Florida's Exotic Fish and Wildlife.* Retrieved from: http://myfwc.com/ wildlifehabitats/nonnatives/

Florida Fish and Wildlife Conservation Commission (FWC, 1999). *Walking catfish.* Retrieved from: http://myfwc.com/wildlifehabitats/profiles/ freshwater/nonnatives/walking-catfish/

Glenn Curtiss Museum (2017). *About the man, Glenn Curtiss museum,* Retrieved from: http://www.glennhcurtissmuseum.org/museum/ glenncurtiss.html

Hall, E. (1959). *The silent language.* Library of Congress Catalog card number 59- 6359. Retrieved from: https://monoskop.org/images/5/57/Hall_ Edward_T_The_Silent_Language.pdf

Kane, A. (2011). Arthritis Foundation. *How fat affects arthritis,* Retrieved from: http://www.arthritis.org/living-with-arthritis/comorbidities/ obesity-arthritis/fat-and-arthritis.php

MacLeod, S. (2014). Simply Psychology, *Personality, type A.* Retrieved from: http://www.simplypsychology.org/personality-a.html

Miller, A.E., MacDougall, J.D., Tarnopolsky, M.A., & Sale, D.G. (1993). European Journal of Applied Physiology and Occupational Physiology. March 1993, Volume 66, Issue 3, pp 254–262. *Gender differences in strength and muscle fiber characteristics.* 66(3):254–262. DOI: https:// doi.org/10.1007/BF00235103

Mirth and Madness (1998). Retrieved from: http://www.mrmd.com/ mir/german.html

National Fire Protection Association (NFPA), Reproduced from NFPA's website, © NFPA (2022), www.nfpa.org/

National Weather Service Forecasting Office, U.S. Department of Commerce, National Weather Service (NWS, 2005). Retrieved from: http://www.srh.noaa.gov/mfl/?n=andrew

Noel, A., Gloviczki, P., Cherry, K., Bower, T., Panneton, J., Geza, M... Hallett, J. (2001). Journal of Vascular Surgery, Vol. 34. Issue 1, July 2001. *Ruptured abdominal aortic aneurysms: The excessive mortality rate of conventional repair.* Retrieved from: https://www.sciencedirect.com/ science/article/pii/S0741521401532000#!

Stanley, I, Hom, M., & Joiner, T. (2016). *A systematic review of suicidal thoughts and behaviors among police officers, firefighters, EMTs, and paramedics.* Clinical psychology review, 44, 25-44.

Phillips, G. (2012). Out of the Shadows: Expanding the Canon of Classic Film Noir. Scarecrow Press. p. 138. ISBN 0810881896. *Retrieved 11 June 2017*

Reh, J. (2016). About Money. *Pareto's principle - the 80-20 rule,* http://management.about.com/cs/generalmanagement/a/Pareto081202.htm

Revolvy (2014). Motorola APCOR. Retrieved from: https://www.revolvy.com/main/index.php?s=Motorola%20APCOR

Star Trek (1982). *The wrath of Khan.* Star Trek, p.120

The Great City of Opa-Locka (2006). *City of Opa-Locka history.* Retrieved from: http://www.opalockafl.gov/index.aspx?nid=229

Thietart, R. A., Forgues, B. (1995). Organizational Science, Vol. 6, Issue 1. *Chaos theory and organization.* Retrieved from: https://s3.amazonaws.com/academia.edu.documents/41874772/Chaos_Theory_and_Organization20160201-1091-1j6c4zk.pdf?AWSAccessKeyId=AKIAIWOWYYGZ2Y53UL3A&Expires=1515352649-&Signature=b%2BWc%2FIItii7v2MM%2FQdaPm2HoWRY%3D&response-content-disposition=inline%3B%20filename%3DChaos_Theory_and_Organization.pdf

United States Department of Agriculture (2016). Animal and Plant Health Inspection Service. *The giant African snail.* Retrieved from: http://www.hungrypests.com/the-threat/giant-african-snail.php

ABOUT THE
AUTHOR

Bob Palestrant has over 40 years of experience in public service serving as a registered nurse, firefighter/paramedic, emergency manager, and in the discipline of homeland security. He is a Certified Emergency Manager (CEM) through the International Association of Emergency Managers (IAEM), a credentialed Chief Fire Officer (CFO) through the Center of Public Safety Excellence, and earned his master's degree in Homeland Security graduating cum laude from American Military University. He has multiple Incident Command System (ICS) instructor certifications, is an Office for Bombing Prevention (OBP) Bomb Making Materials Awareness Program (BMAP) Administrator/Trainer, and a State of Florida Fire Service Instructor III.

After promoting through the ranks, he retired from Miami-Dade Fire Rescue (MDFR) in 2012. During his 28-year career with MDFR, he established and served as the first Chief of the Domestic Preparedness Division, developed and managed the Terrorism Response Bureau, the Tactical Paramedic and Rapid Deployment Force programs, and was responsible for all Homeland Security-related issues and management of major events, including serving as a member of Unified Command for Superbowl XLI and XLIV.

As a member of the Florida Task Force 1 Urban Search and Rescue (US&R) team, he was on several deployments including the World Trade Center attack on 9/11. He was a member of multiple regional, state, and national homeland security-related committees and work groups, including the South East Florida Regional Domestic Security Task Force (SERDSTF), serving as the Terrorism Liaison Officer (TLO) Program Coordinator from 2008-2022.

During his career, Bob also served as Fire Chief at Miami International Airport (MIA), Administrative Division Chief for Operations, Operations District Chief, and Director of the Office of Emergency Management and Homeland Security (OEM&HS) for Miami-Dade County, Florida. As Director of OEM&HS, he coordinating multi-agency and multi-jurisdictional responses to disasters and large-scale emergencies, and as a member of a coalition of Emergency Managers from the 11 largest U.S. cities, worked with the Council of Excellence in Government to standardize and improve methods of increasing the preparedness and the ability of cities to respond to disasters on a national basis.

In 2013, he joined the Broward County Sheriff's Office Department of Fire & Rescue (BSODFRES) as the District Chief at the Ft. Lauderdale/Hollywood International Airport, and was part of Unified Command for two major aircraft incidents and the 2017 mass shooting.

Bob has received multiple service awards and honors, and in 2021, was selected as the Government Technology & Services Coalition-Homeland Security Today's State Homeland Security Person of the Year. He was a technical consultant for the show "Without Warning," broadcast on both The Discovery and The Learning Channels and has been a panel member or given presentations on emergency management, aircraft rescue and firefighting, and homeland security issues at multiple conferences and symposiums across the country and abroad.